G000055742

WALKS IN THE
CEVENNES

Titles in the Footpaths of Europe Series

The publishers thank the following people for permission to use their
photographs in this book: J. Cantaloube, C. Fantola, H. Viaux.

WALKS IN THE
CEVENNES

Translated by John Maddison
and Daphne Terry

Robertson McCarta

The publishers thank the following people for their help with this book: Isabelle
Daguin, Philippe Lambert, Serge Sineux.

First published in 1991 by

Robertson McCarta Limited
17-18 Angel Gate
City Road
London EC1V 2PT

in association with

Fédération Française de la Randonnée Pédestre
8 Avenue Marceau
75008 Paris

© Robertson McCarta Limited
© Fédération Française de Randonnée Pédestre
© Maps, Institut Geographique National (French Official Survey)
   and Robertson McCarta Limited.

Managing Editor Folly Marland
Series designed by Prue Bucknall
Production by Grahame Griffiths
Typeset by The Robertson Group, Llandudno
Origination by Toppan Limited
Planning Map by Rodney Paull

Printed and bound in Italy by Grafedit S.p.A, Bergamo.

British Library Cataloguing in Publication Data

Walks in the Cévennes. – (Footpaths of Europe).
   1. France – Visitors' guides
   I. Series
   914.48

   ISBN 1-85365-233-4

Every care has been taken to ensure that all the information in this
book is accurate. The publishers cannot accept any responsibility
for any errors that may appear or their consequences.

CONTENTS

The walks and maps

Walk 1 *(Tour du Mont Lozère)*

GR68 Villefort ▶ Bagnols-les-Bains ▶ La Loubière ▶ Florac
▶ Croix de Berthel ▶ Genolhac ▶ Concoules ▶ Villefort
GR7 Le Bleymard

Walk 2 *(Tour en Pays Cévenol - the Gardons Valleys)*

GR67 Anduze ▶ Colognac ▶ Aire-de-Côte ▶ Barre-des-Cévennes
▶ Saint-André de Lancize ▶ Mialet ▶ Anduze
GR67A Mont Mars ▶ Saint-Germain-de-Calberte ▶ Pierre de la Vieille
GR67B Les Ayres ▶ Le Pendédis ▶ Le Pradel, and Canteloup
▶ Pierre de la Vieille
GR63 and GR6A Detour Lasalle
GR6B and GR6C Detour Notre-Dame-de-la-Rouvière

Walk 3 *(Tour du Mont Aigoual)*

GR66 L'Espérou ▶ Col de l'Homme Mort ▶ Dourbies ▶ Meyrueis
▶ Cabrillac ▶ Aire-de-Côte ▶ Mont Aigoual ▶ L'Espérou
GR66A and GR62 Alternative route Col du Suquet ▶ Camprieu
▶ Abîme de Bramabiau ▶ Pierre Plantée

Key to IGN Maps

Motorway, dual carriageway

Major road, four lanes or more

Main road, two-lane or three-lane, wide

Main road, two-lane, narrow

Narrow road, regularly surfaced

Other narrow road: regularly surfaced; irregularly surfaced

Possibly private or controlled access

Field track, forest track, felling track, footpath

Track of disused road. Road under construction

Road through embankment, cutting. Tree-lined road or track

Bank, Hedge, line of trees

Railway: double track, single track. Electrified line. Station, waiting line. Halt, stop

Sidings or access lines. Narrow gauge line. Rack railway

Electricity transmission line. Cable railway. Ski lift

National boundary with markers

Boundary and administrative centre of department, district

PF   SP

Boundary and administrative centre of canton, commune

CT   C

For shooting times, go to town hall or gendarmerie

Boundary of military camp, firing range

Boundary of State forest, National Park, outer zone of National Park

Triangulation points

Church, chapel, shrine. Cross, tomb, religious statue. Cemetery

Watch tower, fortress. Windmill, wind-pump. Chimney

Tr   Chem.

Storage tank: oil, gas. Blast furnace. Pylon. Quarry

Cave. Monument, pillar. Castle. Ruins

Mon.

Megalithic monument: dolmen, menhir. Viewpoint. Campsite

P.V.

Market-hall, shed, glasshouse, casemate

Access to underground workings. Refuge. Ski-jump

Mine   Cave

Population/thousands

183,2   0,4   0,15   0,06

Bridge. Footbridge. Ford. Ferry

Lake, pool. Area liable to flooding. Marsh

Source, spring. Well, water-tank. Water-tower, reservoir

Ch.
d'Eau

Watercourse lined with trees. Waterfall. Dam. Dyke

Navigable canal, feeder or irrigator. Lock, machine-operated. Underground channel

Contour lines. 10 m. interval. Hollow. Small basin. Scree

| Woodland | Scrub | Orchard, plantation | Vines | Ricefield |

All maps are IGN Orange series. 1:50 000

© I.G.N. – Paris

A note from the publisher

The books in this French Walking Guide series are produced in association and with the help of the Fédération Française de la Randonnée Pédestre (French ramblers' association) — generally known as the FFRP.

The FFRP is a federal organisation and is made up of regional, local and many other associations and bodies that form its constituent parts. Individual membership is through these various local organisations. The FFRP therefore acts as an umbrella organisation overseeing the waymarking of footpaths, training and the publishing of the Topoguides, detailed guides to the Grande Randonnée footpaths.

There are at present about 170 Topoguides in print, compiled and written by local members of the FFRP, who are responsible for waymarking the walks — so they are well researched and accurate.

We have translated the main itinerary descriptions, amalgamating and adapting several Topoguides to create new regional guides. We have retained the basic Topoguide structure, indicating length and times of walks, and the Institut Géographique National (official French survey) maps overlaid with the routes.

The information contained in this guide is the latest available at the time of going to print. However, as publishers we are aware that this kind of information is continually changing and we are anxious to enhance and improve the guides as much as possible. We encourage you to send us suggestions, criticisms and those little bits of information you may wish to share with your fellow walkers. Our address is: Robertson McCarta, 17-18 Angel Gate, City Road, London EC1V 2PT.

We shall be happy to offer a free copy of any one of these books to any reader whose suggestions are subsequently incorporated into a new edition.

It is possible to create a variety of routes by referring to the walks in the contents page and to the planning map (inside the front cover). Transport is listed in the alphabetical index in the back of the book and there is an accommodation guide.

The full range of IGN (French OS) maps is available from The Map and Guide Shop, who operate a mail order service, 17-18 Angel Gate, City Road, London EC1V 2PT, Tel: 071 278 8276

KEY

Gournay

This example shows that you can expect the walk from Gournay to Arbois to take 2 hours, 10 minutes.

2:10

ARBOIS

🏠 ⌂ ✕ ⚖ 🚃

14th century church

Arbois has a variety of facilities, including hotels and buses. Hotel addresses and bus/train connections may be listed in the index at the back of the book.

A grey arrow indicates an alternative route that leaves and returns to the main route.

Detour

indicates a short detour off the route to a town with facilities or to an interesting sight.

Symbols

🏠 hotel
⌂ youth hostel, hut or refuge
🅰 camping
✕ restaurant
🍸 café

⚖ shops
🚇 railway station
🚌 buses
⛴ ferry
🅱 tourist information

THE FOOTPATHS OF FRANCE

by Robin Neillands

Why should you go walking in France? Well, walking is fun and as for France, Danton summed up the attractions of that country with one telling phrase: 'Every man has two countries,' he said, 'his own . . . and France.' That is certainly true in my case and I therefore consider it both a pleasure and an honour to write this general introduction to these footpath guides to France. A pleasure because walking in or through France is my favourite pastime, an honour because these excellent English language guides follow in the course set by those Topo-guides published in French by the Fédération Française pour la Randonnée Pédestre, which set a benchmark for quality that all footpath guides might follow. Besides, I believe that good things should be shared and walking in France is one of the most pleasant activities I know.

I have been walking in France for over thirty years. I began by rambling — or rather ambling — through the foothills of the Pyrenees, crossing over into Spain past the old Hospice de France, coming back over the Somport Pass in a howling blizzard, which may account for the fact that I totally missed two sets of frontier guards on both occasions. Since then I have walked in many parts of France and even from one end of it to the other, from the Channel to the Camargue, and I hope to go on walking there for many years to come.

The attractions of France are legion, but there is no finer way to see and enjoy them than on foot. France has two coasts, at least three mountain ranges — the Alps, Pyrenees and the Massif Central — an agreeable climate, a great sense of space, good food, fine wines and, believe it or not, a friendly and hospitable people. If you don't believe me, go there on foot and see for yourself. Walking in France will appeal to every kind of walker, from the day rambler to the backpacker, because above all, and in the nicest possible way, the walking in France is well organised, but those Francophiles who already know France well will find it even more pleasurable if they explore their favourite country on foot.

The GR system

The Grande Randonnée (GR) footpath network now consists of more than 40,000 kilometres (25,000 miles) of long-distance footpath, stretching into every part of France, forming a great central sweep around Paris, probing deeply into the Alps, the Pyrenees, and the volcanic cones of the Massif Central. This network, the finest system of footpaths in Europe, is the creation of that marvellously named organisation, *la Fédération Française de Randonnée Pédestre, Comité National des Sentiers de Grande Randonnée,* which I shall abbreviate to FFRP-CNSGR. Founded in 1948, and declaring that, *'un jour de marche, huit jours de santé'* the FFRP-CNSGR has flourished for four decades and put up the now familiar red-and-white waymarks in every corner of the country. Some of these footpaths are classic walks, like the famous GR65, *Le Chemin de St Jacques,* the ancient Pilgrim Road to Compostela, the TMB, the *Tour du Mont Blanc,* which circles the mountain through France, Switzerland and Italy, or the 600-mile long GR3, the *Sentier de la Loire,* which runs from the Ardèche to the Atlantic, to give three examples from the hundred or so GR trails available. In addition there is an abundance of GR du Pays or regional footpaths, like the *Sentier de la Haute Auvergne*, and the *Sentier Tour des Monts d'Aubrac*. A 'Tour' incidentally, is usually a circular walk. Many of these regional or provincial GR trails are charted and waymarked in red-and-yellow by local outdoor organisations such as ABRI (Association Bretonne des Relais et Itineraires) for Brittany, or CHAMINA for the Massif Central. The walker in France will soon become familiar with all these footpath networks, national, regional or local, and find them the perfect way into the heart and heartland of France. As a little bonus, the GR networks are expanding all the time, with the detours — or *variantes* — off the main route eventually linking with other GR paths or *variantes* and becoming GR trails in their own right.

Walkers will find the GR trails generally well marked and easy to follow, and they have two advantages over the footpaths commonly encountered in the UK. First, since they are laid out by local people, they are based on intricate local knowledge of the local sights. If there is a fine view, a mighty castle or a pretty village on your footpath route, your footpath through France will surely lead you to it. Secondly, all French footpaths are usually well provided with a wide range of comfortable country accommodation, and you will discover that the local people, even the farmers, are well used to walkers and greet them with a smile, a *'Bonjour'* and a *'Bonne route'*.

Terrain and Climate

As a glance at these guides or any Topoguide will indicate, France has a great variety of terrain. France is twice the size of the UK and many natural features are also on a larger scale. There are three main ranges of mountains, the Alps contain the highest mountain in Europe, the Pyrenees go up to 10,000 ft, the Massif Central peaks to over 6000 ft, and there are many similar ranges with hills which overtop our highest British peak, Ben Nevis. On the other hand, the Auvergne and the Jura have marvellous open ridge walking, the Cévennes are steep and rugged, the Ardèche and parts of Provence are hot and wild, the Île de France, Normandy, Brittany and much of Western France is green and pleasant, not given to extremes. There is walking in France for every kind of walker, but given such a choice the wise walker will consider the complications of terrain and weather before setting out, and go suitably equipped.

France enjoys three types of climate: continental, oceanic, and mediterranean. South of the Loire it will certainly be hot to very hot from mid-April to late September. Snow can fall on the mountains above 4000 ft from mid-October and last until May, or even lie year-round on the tops and in couloirs; in the high hills an ice-axe is never a frill. I have used one by the Brèche de Roland in the Pyrenees in mid-June.

Wise walkers should study weather maps and forecasts carefully in the week before they leave for France, but can generally expect good weather from May to October, and a wide variety of weather — the severity depending on the terrain — from mid-October to late Spring.

Accommodation

The walker in France can choose from a wide variety of accommodation with the asurance that the walker will always be welcome. This can range from country hotels to wild mountain pitches, but to stay in comfort, many walkers will travel light and overnight in the comfortable hotels of the *Logis de France* network.

Logis de France: The *Logis de France* is a nationwide network of small, family-run country hotels, offering comfortable accommodation and excellent food. *Logis* hotels are graded and can vary from a simple, one-star establishment, with showers and linoleum, to a four- or five-star *logis* with gastronomic menus and deep-pile carpets. All offer excellent value for money, and since there are over 5,000 scattered across the French countryside, they provide a good focus for a walking day. An annual guide to the *Logis* is available from the French Government Tourist Office, 178 Piccadilly, London W1V 0AL, Tel (071) 491 7622.

Gîtes d'étape: A *gîte d'étape* is best imagined as an unmanned youth hostel for outdoor folk of all ages. They lie along the footpath networks and are usually signposted or listed in the guides. They can be very comfortable, with bunk beds, showers, a well equipped kitchen, and in some cases they have a warden, a *guardien*, who may offer meals. *Gîtes d'étape* are designed exclusively for walkers, climbers, cyclists, cross country skiers or horse-riders. A typical price (1990) would be Fr.25 for one night. *Gîtes d'étape* should not be confused with a *Gîte de France*. A *gîte* — usually signposted as '*Gîte de France*' — is a country cottage available for a holiday let, though here too, the owner may be more than willing to rent it out as overnight accommodation.

Youth hostels: Curiously enough, there are very few Youth Hostels in France outside the main towns. A full list of the 200 or so available can be obtained from the Youth Hostel Association (YHA), Trevelyan House, St. Albans, Herts AL1 2DY.

Pensions or cafés: In the absence of an hotel, a *gîte d'étape* or a youth hostel, all is not lost. France has plenty of accommodation and an enquiry at the village café or bar will usually produce a room. The café/hotel may have rooms or suggest a nearby pension or a *chambre d'hôte*. Prices start at around Fr.50 for a room, rising to say, Fr.120. (1990 estimate).

Chambres d'hôte: A *chambre d'hôte* is a guest room, or, in English terms, a bed-and-breakfast, usually in a private house. Prices range from about Fr.60 a night. *Chambres d'hôte* signs are now proliferating in the small villages of France and especially if you can speak a little French are an excellent way to meet the local people. Prices (1990) are from, say, Fr.70 for a room, not per person.

Abris: *Abris*, shelters or mountain huts can be found in the mountain regions, where they are often run by the Club Alpin Français, an association for climbers. They range from the comfortable to the primitive, are often crowded and are sometimes reserved for members. Details from the Club Alpin Français, 7 Rue la Boétie, Paris 75008, France.

Camping: French camp sites are graded from one to five star, but are generally very good at every level, although the facilities naturally vary from one cold tap to shops, bars and heated pools. Walkers should not be deterred by the '*Complet*' (Full) sign on the gate or office window: a walker's small tent will usually fit in somewhere. *Camping à la ferme*, or farm camping, is increasingly popular, more primitive — or less regimented — than the official sites, but widely available and perfectly adequate. Wild camping is officially not permitted in National Parks, but unofficially if you are over 1,500m away from a road, one hour's walk from a *gîte* or camp site, and where possible ask permission, you should have no trouble. French country people will always assist the walker to find a pitch.

The law for walkers

The country people of France seem a good deal less concerned about their 'rights' than the average English farmer or landowner. I have never been ordered off land in France or greeted with anything other than friendliness . . . maybe I've been lucky. As a rule, walkers in France are free to roam over all open paths and tracks. No decent walker will leave gates open, trample crops or break down walls, and taking fruit from gardens or orchards is simply stealing. In some parts of France there are local laws about taking chestnuts, mushrooms (and snails), because these are cash crops. Signs like *Réserve de Chasse,* or *Chasse Privé* indicate that the shooting is reserved for the landowner. As a general rule, behave sensibly and you will be tolerated everywhere, even on private land.

The country code

Walkers in France should obey the *Code du Randonneur.*

- Love and respect nature.
- Avoid unnecessary noise.
- Destroy nothing.
- Do not leave litter.
- Do not pick flowers or plants.
- Do not disturb wildlife.
- Re-close all gates.
- Protect and preserve the habitat.
- No smoking or fires in the forests. (This rule is essential and is actively enforced by foresters and police.)
- Respect and understand the country way of life and the country people.
- Think of others as you think of yourself.

Transport

Transportation to and within France is generally excellent. There are no less than nine Channel ports: Dunkirk, Calais, Boulogne, Dieppe, Le Havre, Caen/Ouistreham, Cherbourg, Saint-Malo and Roscoff, and a surprising number of airports served by direct flights from the UK. Although some of the services are seasonal, it is often possible to fly direct to Toulouse, Poitiers, Nantes, Perpignan, Montpellier, indeed to many provincial cities, as well as Paris and such obvious destinations as Lyon and Nice. Within France the national railway, the SNCF, still retains a nationwide network. Information, tickets and a map can be obtained from the SNCF. France also has a good country bus service and the *gare routière* is often placed just beside the railway station. Be aware though, that many French bus services only operate within the *département,* and they do not generally operate from one provincial city to the next. I cannot encourage people to hitch-hike, which is both illegal and risky, but walkers might consider a taxi for their luggage. Almost every French village has a taxi driver who will happily transport your rucksacks to the next night-stop, fifteen to twenty miles away, for Fr.50 a head or even less.

Money

Walking in France is cheap, but banks are not common in the smaller villages, so carry a certain amount of French money and the rest in traveller's cheques or Eurocheques, which are accepted everywhere.

Clothing and equipment

The amount of clothing and equipment you will need depends on the terrain, the length of the walk, the time of your visit, the accommodation used. Outside the mountain areas it is not necessary to take the full range of camping or backpacking gear. I once walked across France from the Channel to the Camargue along the Grande Randonneé footpaths in March, April and early May and never needed to use any of the camping gear I carried in my rucksack because I found hotels everywhere, even in quite small villages.

Essential items are:

In summer: light boots, a hat, shorts, suncream, lip salve, mosquito repellent, sunglasses, a sweater, a windproof cagoule, a small first-aid kit, a walking stick.

In winter: a change of clothing, stormproof outer garments, gaiters, hat, lip salve, a companion.

In the mountains at any time: large-scale maps (1:25,000), a compass, an ice-axe. In winter, add a companion and ten-point crampons.

At any time: a phrase book, suitable maps, a dictionary, a sense of humour.

The best guide to what to take lies in the likely weather and the terrain. France tends to be informal, so there is no need to carry a jacket or something smart for the evenings. I swear by Rohan clothing, which is light, smart and functional. The three things I would never go without are light, well-broken-in boots and several pairs of loop-stitched socks, and my walking stick.

Health hazards

Health hazards are few. France can be hot in summer, so take a full water-bottle and refill at every opportunity. A small first-aid kit is sensible, with plasters and 'mole-skin' for blisters, but since prevention is better than the cure, loop-stitched socks and flexible boots are better. Any French chemist — *a pharmacie* — is obliged to render first-aid treatment for a small fee. These pharmacies can be found in most villages and large towns and are marked by a green cross.

Dogs are both a nuisance and a hazard. All walkers in France should carry a walking stick to fend off aggressive curs. Rabies — *la rage* — is endemic and any one bitten must seek immediate medical advice. France also possesses two types of viper, which are common in the hill areas of the south. In fairness, although I found my walking stick indispensable, I must add that in thirty years I have never even seen a snake or a rabid dog. In case of real difficulty, dial 17 for the police and the ambulance.

Food and wine

One of the great advantages with walking in France is that you can end the day with a good meal and not gain an ounce. French country cooking is generally excellent and good value for money, with the price of a four-course menu starting at about Fr.45. The ingredients for the mid-day picnic can be purchased from the village shops and these also sell wine. Camping-Gaz cylinders and cartridges are widely available, as is 2-star petrol for stoves. Avoid naked fires.

Preparation

The secret of a good walk lies in making adequate preparations before you set out. It pays to be fit enough to do the daily distance at the start. Much of the necessary information is contained in this guide, but if you need more, look in guidebooks or outdoor magazines, or ask friends.

The French

I cannot close this introduction without saying a few words about the French, not least because the walker in France is going to meet rather more French people than, say, a motorist will, and may even meet French people who have never met a foreigner before. It does help if the visitor speaks a little French, even if only to say *'Bonjour'* and *'Merci'* and *'S'il vous plaît'*. The French tend to be formal so it pays to be polite, to say 'hello', to shake hands. I am well aware that relations between France and England have not always been cordial over the last six hundred years or so, but I have never met with hostility of any kind in thirty years of walking through France. Indeed, I have always found that if the visitor is prepared to meet the French halfway, they will come more than halfway to greet him or her in return, and are both friendly and hospitable to the passing stranger.

As a final tip, try smiling. Even in France, or especially in France, a smile and a *'Pouvez vous m'aider?'* (Can you help me?) will work wonders. That's my last bit of advice, and all I need do now is wish you *'Bonne Route'* and good walking in France.

WALKS IN THE CÉVENNES

The Cévennes run from l'Espérou to Mont Lozère by way of Mont Aigoual and the Montagne du Bougès. Most of these high tops, and the Montagne de l'Espérou, the Bonheur valley region, the Can de l'Hospitalet, the Plan de Fontmort, the Mas de la Barque, consist of broad grassy saddles separating wide flat-bottomed valleys, that are peaty and damp where the rock is granitic or schist, dry where limestone prevails, and everywhere good grazing.

But the close proximity of the Mediterranean acts as an immediate and irresistible attraction for every least trickle of water. Rivulets quickly turn into torrents, carving out deep and precipitous channels through narrow rocky valleys, and the rough stream beds where trout dart to and fro are broken at intervals by cataracts and turbulent 'giant's cauldron' pot-holes. Rushing headlong down, these *'gardons'* cut perpendicular ravines in the mountainside, leaving none of the smooth surface we found on the heights, but a series of sharp spurs and ridges, the Cévenol 'Serres', running down towards the plain.

They are all alike, these valleys, with their soils of ancient siliceous and crystalline schists, dark reds, violets, blues – all sombre colours. But three stand out: the Vallée Française, Vallée Longue and Vallée Borgne, running down in parallel towards the woodland below. And the cols too, Col Salidès, Col du Marquairès, Col de Jalcreste and many others where the ancient roads pass, and 'tiered' shelves and ledges witness to how these old valley beds are continually being dug deeper.

Today the destructive force of these mountain torrents is enormous. Their flash floods, the *'gardonnades'*, are rightly feared by the people who live beside them: they rise in spate very suddenly: two or three days of rain, which falls more heavily here than almost anywhere else in France, and the narrow valleys are inundated. The waters rise and instantly fields are flooded, houses destroyed, roads washed away. The steep slopes, and the formidable rainfall brought by the south wind off the sea as it drives up against the mountains, combine to stir up the torrents. These soon overflow their sources, adding to their flood, one day here one one day there, waters that previously emptied into the Atlantic – as one can see especially at l'Espérou, La Serreyrède and the Col des Faïsses.

In these narrow valleys the contrast is very great between the appearance of the south-facing slopes, the sunlit *'adrets'* or *'soleyrols'*, and the shaded north-facing *'avès'* or *'ubacs'*.

On the shaded flanks one sees here and there, from the summits right down to the rivers, piled-up heaps of earth and rough fragments of schist. These were formed thousands of years ago when ice and intense cold stretched as far as the Mediterranean, and then when the thaw came and the ice melted, it carried earth and stones down the mountainsides. On the valley bottoms and sunny slopes Mediterranean-type vegetation pushed long fingers of green up towards the watershed. Above the fields and orchards irrigated by small canals called *'béais'*, and above the gardens or *'horts'*, are little walled terraces, the *'bancels'* or *'faïsses'* where olives and

15

vines, mulberries and figs are grown.

On the rocky slopes where sheep wander and goats are happiest, there are woods of holm-oak mingled with tall heaths, broom, arbutus, juniper and a tangle of creepers – a veritable *maquis.*

But Lord of the Cévennes, a staple source of food and wealth, is the Spanish chestnut, growing everywhere, from the river banks where it flourishes best, up to the high summits where it tends to decline. In the past chestnut trees covered the whole range, up to a height of 800m, with a blanket unbroken except for narrow strips where the *drailles,* or transhumance routes, had torn an open path for the seasonal movement of livestock, and clearings for the *clèdes,* like small square oast-houses, where the chestnuts were dried. In these mountains the chestnut tree was King – with chestnuts, pork, a little corn, Clinton wine and their garden produce, the Cévenol people lacked nothing, they said, except salt. But times have changed and barren heathland makes increasing inroads into the chestnut forests. Factories producing the tanning agents extracted from the bark have as inexorable an effect on the forests as the flood levels have on the ever deepening stream beds.

Above 800m the chestnut plantations end, and the beech prevails. Throughout the Aigoual massif, and also the Lozère and Bougès ranges, there are splendid forests of serried beeches and scattered rowans, with beautiful clearings where gentians and arnica grow. And in a remote corner of Lozère there are still a few very old silver firs, descendants, maybe, of ancient fir-woods now gone, witnessing perhaps, like the screes in the Palhères valley, to the existence of glaciers in Cévenol during the Quaternary ice-age.

It was to restore these forests, both on Mont Aigoual and the Lozère range, that forestry experts under the leadership of Georges Fabre spent so much time and trouble. And it is the result of their efforts, as well as the natural beauty of this landscape, which make a tour of the Aigoual, especially, so interesting, as typical of the whole Cévennes region.

A soil of schist, dusty and permeable on the surface but becoming waterlogged in the autumn rains, gives rise to numerous springs. The intense heat of summer reduces their flow but rarely dries them up. This is why, apart from some larger valley villages like Saint-André-de-Valborgne, Sainte-Croix-de-Vallée Française, Le Collet de Dèze-en-Vallongue, the Cévennes map is black with the placenames of small-holdings and farmhouses scattered over the countryside or grouped into little hamlets. On almost any flat shelf or mountain shoulder stands the tall house beside a mossy flower-fringed spring. Its walls are great rough-hewn blocks of dark schist or white quartz, its lintels of micaceous rock, roofed with *lauzes,* thick slabs or shingles of schist. Alongside, close to the garden, are two or three tombstones – the family graveyard. Inside, by the hearth, where dried chestnuts are cooking, we shall find some old bent woman, dressed in black, and perhaps a little boy and girl in sabots, with cheeks as red as the autumn cherries on the tree outside. Polite and shy, they will grow up to become perhaps a farm bailiff, a headmistress of a local school. For many of the Cévenol people emigrate to other valleys or to the towns – they have always done so, and many of the farmhouses, especially the higher ones, have fallen into ruin. They leave in droves, these Cévenols – serious and determined workers who prosper wherever they go. They only come home in the dog-days, when the valley plains are sweltering and small children pine in the fiery heat. At that season the mountain villages – l'Espérou, Pompidou, Vialas – turn into summer resorts, and are bursting with people.

Finally, before leaving that peaceful dwelling, take a look at the old engravings on the wall: portraits of Huguenots with their square caps and long beards – Calvin or

Luther perhaps, among others – celebrating the Reformation. For this is a land where the Wars of Religion were fought, and battles and uprisings and oppression took place – a land of pastors and prophets, of the 'Psalm beneath the stars', of 'Roux the Bandit' who only yesterday, in time of turmoil, pitted his faith against the law. This is a land of free spirits, where the printed word is read and discussed; but where ancient legends also abound. At night, when the 'sea-wind' hurls the rain against the small panes of narrow windows, the chestnut pickers retell the tale of 'Jean de l'Hort', or the one about the farmer's wife who was a witch and traced a magic circle to protect her poultry against the fox.

So do not despise our modest yet glorious Cévennes. Make your way up to Mont Aigoual on foot, along the ancient sheep-tracks of the drailles, from Anduze to Meyrueis or from Barre to Vigan. You will find them strewn with dolmens, fallen menhirs and sacrificial stones, the traces of prehistoric transhumance, of flocks led by early iron-age shepherds who left their flints and shards behind them when they halted at the Col de l'Homme Mort in the Lingas.

And explore the heights of Mont Lozère – all too little known; follow the Corniche des Cévennes that runs from Saint-Jean-du-Gard to Le Pompidou; return to Barre by way of the Can de l'Hospitalet. Between the Gorges du Tarn and the Garrigues to the south, spend a few days in the Cévennes: enjoy the wide horizons of the summits and nostalgic charm of the valleys. This will soon become the land where you most wish to be, and that little house of an earlier age, screened in its grove of walnut and ash, will become the house that you wish was your own.

PAUL MARCELLIN
Honorary Curator of the Museum of Natural History, Nîmes

THE 'DRAILLES'

Old dictionaries of the *'langue d'Oc'* – the Oc or Occitan dialect still spoken by some of the country people – define *'drailles'* as 'sheep tracks, and especially those regularly used for the seasonal transhumance of flocks from the valley farms to summer pastures in the mountains'.

How Drailles were formed

These drailles, some of which are 20 metres wide and marked out by standing stones or edged with low drystone walls, take the shortest possible route, climbing from col to col and often scaling precipitous slopes. They began as prehistoric forerunners of the regular paths used by the mountain people over the centuries. They were doubtless first created by the wild sheep, mouflon, deer, cattle, horses and pigs living in total freedom before man the hunter had thought of domesticating them. Driven from the southern plains by heat and drought, they came up at the start of each summer to look for green grass and coolth in the mountains, to Mont Lozère, the Margeride, Aubrac. Then when the first frosts arrived they went down again to the sheltered lowlands.

During these journeys they quite naturally followed the open ridges, avoiding the tangled thickets of the lower slopes and valley bottoms. And so the yearly trampling of these flocks and herds ended by tracing very direct routes linking the plains with the mountains. And at times when the animals were on the move the hunters of prehistory came to frequent the ridgeways looking for the game they needed, and so learnt of the route and the season of migration.

Then in the Neolithic age, perhaps some 8,000 years BC, sheep became domesticated and men became shepherds; and led by their flocks rather than leading them, they joined the instinctive transhumance of their sheep, following the tracks the animals had created. But with domestication the animals lost their instinct, and the shepherds led the way, still following the old routes, the drailles. And as time went on, besides the sheep and shepherds, all sorts of travellers, peasants and pedlars, pilgrims and tramps, were using the drailles all the year round. For them, with leg muscles of steel from moving up and down the steep hillsides with produce and stores, the narrow tracks with their marker stones to show the way in winter snows, and rough causeways to give a firmer footing on marshy ground, were highway enough.

Later on, when mules were used for carrying heavy loads, they could not manage the steepest parts of the drailles, so less rugged paths had to be found, with bends on the steeper slopes; thus separate mule tracks were created. And then with the coming of large carts drawn by oxen or horses the mule tracks had to be widened and slopes made gentler to prevent the wagons over-turning; so the tracks became roads, in many places following the valley bottoms and not the ridges. But the migrating sheep continued to use the drailles.

Three main routes linked – and still link – the lower Languedoc valleys with the summer pastures:

The **Draille du Gévaudan,** or du Languedoc, runs from the Anduze region up to the Montagne de la Vieille Morte, then via the cols of Jalcreste, La Croix de Berthel and Finiels on through Le Bleymard and across the Montagne du Goulet.

The **Draille de la Margeride** enables flocks from Bas-Languedoc to reach the Mont Lozère pastures by way of Colognac, Aire-de-Côte, La Can de l'Hospitalet and Florac. It crosses the Lozère range, passing near the Croix de Maître Vidal, and reaches the River Lot at Chadenet.

The **Draille d'Aubrac,** or Grande Draille, is used by flocks from the Montpellier region, which re-group near Notre-Dame-de-Londres for the journey on toward Ganges, the Col des Mourèzes, Cap-de-Côte and La Lusette. Then, via La Serreyrède, Cabrillac and Perjuret, towards the Causse de Méjean, it crosses the River Tarn at Sainte-Énimie and the Lot at Le Pont-de-Salmon, before starting the climb up towards Aubrac in company with the GR60.

The Flock on the Draille

The flocks start their journey up to the mountains somewhere between 1 and 15 June. Several flocks, totalling up to 3,000 animals, depart together, attended by several shepherds and their dogs. The pace is unhurried, perhaps 2.5 to 3 kilometres an hour, in daily stages of 20 to 25 kilometres. To make the most of the morning coolth, the flock leaves each camping place by dawn, sometimes even while it is still dark.

Where there is grazing alongside the draille, the shepherds slow the pace, to give the sheep time to browse. As the drailles mostly follow the ridges, there will be few watering places, and the flocks may go several days without a drink. At midday, when heat is greatest, there is a halt and a siesta; and the march resumes about 4 o'clock and continues till dusk. The flock is then driven into a pen for the night. The whole journey lasts five to six days.

For the journey down to the plains again the flock is divided in two. A first contingent, consisting of the lambs and any lame or sick animals, departs somewhere between 15 August and 8 September, leaving the adults to descend later, around 20 September.

Decline of the Drailles

In the past 200 years transhumance has declined drastically, for a number of reasons. Large areas of mountain grazing have been reforested, or switched to agriculture or other stock than sheep. In the lowlands, now given over to intensive vine-growing and fruit-farming, many of the smaller flocks have disappeared. The number of shepherds is diminishing too: young people today are not attracted by the rough conditions and the three-month long isolation in the mountains. And increased motor traffic and tourism hamper the large-scale movement of sheep, and disturb their stay in the mountains; so many of the Languedoc flocks stay down on the farms all the year round. Although some thousands of sheep do still make the annual journey, their numbers today are tiny compared with the hundreds of thousands using the drailles even in the mid-19th century. Deserted and neglected, the lines of the drailles are becoming blurred in many places; by the early 1980s the Draille d'Aubrac was totally abandoned, and some people think they may disappear altogether.

PROTESTANTISM AND THE CAMISARD WAR

The surprising level of culture among Cévenol people owes much to their Protestantism, even though elsewhere too a mountain environment seems to encourage learning – as in the Hautes Alpes, traditional source of the nation's schoolmasters. To read the Bible for yourself you need to be literate! One sign of this culture is a taste for reading: simple peasants discussing works of erudition. Even in very poor homes they keep and care for a small library; 'Here no one throws books away', they say. People also treasure old documents: the written word is seen as something sacred, and one may find quite modest families keeping papers that date back to the 17th and 18th centuries, if not earlier.

Protestantism and religious resistance have moreover profoundly influenced the social development of the region, especially in the political sphere. The local form of republicanism originated in the structures of the Reformed Church, which organised itself in complete independence from the social hierarchy of the time, and in opposition to established authority. And this experience of religious democracy prepared the Cévennes for non-conformity on political democracy. Protestantism also in the end forced the Cévenol community to open itself to the rest of the world – with cultural and religious imperatives reinforcing economic necessity. At a quite early date this small enclave began to play a part in the general European scene, and Cévenol people today are discovering distant cousins who left the region three centuries ago and are now returning to look for their roots. The prestige of the region is great, and not only among French or foreign Protestants; for many people it symbolises the victory of the 'little flock' of Israel over the powers of this world.

'Children of God': the Prophets and the Camisards

Faced by increasingly ferocious repression of their preachers, the Cévenol people took refuge in flights of fancy. Arriving from the Vivarais in 1700, their 'prophets' travelled through the valleys calling people to repent and to leave 'Babylon' (the Catholic Church) behind them, and proclaiming the re-establishment of Protestantism in all its glory.

This show of resistance, sometimes leading to outbreaks of mass hysteria, brought further persecution, and the 'prophesying' which had started as a quite peaceful movement, now turned to violence. The 'War of the Camisards' began in 1702 with the assassination of the Abbé du Chayla, inspector of missions, at Le Pont de Montvert. For two years, fewer than 2,000 peasants and artisans held out against more than 25,000 regular troops, in a true guerrilla warfare, prefiguring the revolutionary wars of our own twentieth century. Deportations, forcible resettlements of population, even the burning down of more than 400 villages, were all of no avail. Only after the arms supply of one

Camisard leader, Jean Cavalier, had been captured, and another leader, Roland, treacherously killed, was calm gradually restored to the region.

Louis XV was no more successful than his predecessor. Resistance continued in the Cévennes, but by this time the monarchy went about the business of repression more prudently. Eventually, by about 1760, a degree of tolerance had been effected, and this was officially recognised in 1787. But the century-long resistance had a deep and lasting effect on the Cévenol countryside and the soul of its people.

PH. JOUTARD

The word 'Camisard' appeared for the first time in 1702, in a private letter, and was adopted in official correspondence shortly afterwards. What was the origin of this name, given to the insurgents of the Cévennes? Several answers have been offered. Jean Cavalier explained in his memoirs that as they were continually moving around the mountains with little opportunity to change their linen, they were only too glad of the passing chance to snatch a shirt or two from clothes-lines in the gardens of the bourgeoisie. The jibe 'camisards' or 'shirt-stealers' thus became a title of honour, rather as the nickname 'Gueux' meaning 'ragamuffins' was adopted by Protestants in revolt against Spanish rule in the Netherlands. The Camisard prophet Abraham Mazel gave a different answer: 'Our clothes got in our way, and we took every opportunity of wearing just a shirt or vest (a 'camisole') so as to move about more easily'. Others again derive the name from *'camisarde'*, meaning 'a night attack on the highway' – a frequent tactic in the mountains. The Larousse dictionary, however, plays safe, defining the name in its own right, as simply: 'Cévenol Calvinists who fought against the armies of Louis XIV after the revocation of the Edict of Nantes'.

THE REVIEW CHEMINS,
special number on the Cévennes

Forests of the Cévennes
The Cévenol Forests have a double origin, both natural and 'artificial'.

Natural Forests The Cévennes are the home of the Spanish chestnut, which dominates and gives its particular character to every hillside up to an altitude of 600-800m. The holm-oak is not specific to the Cévennes, but is found in all the valleys, up to 400-500m. Above that it gives way to the white or 'durmast' oak which flourishes up to 800-900m. Higher than that we reach the domain of the beech, but the natural beech forests have been much depleted by human activity. Among conifers, the Scotch or Norway pine appears at almost every level and on all soils, and the Salzmann pine, almost non-existent elsewhere in France, still survives around the Col d'Uglas.

Artificial Forests These consist mainly of a species introduced to the region, the maritime pine, widely used in the 19th century for pit-props. The snow line limits its upper spread to 600m. Other conifers too have been acclimatised in the state forests: spruce, larch, pitch pine, Austrian black pine and the Corsican Laricio.

P. MAGNE

Spanish Chestnuts: Bread from a Tree
'On the lower slopes, and far up every glen, the Spanish chestnut-trees stood each four-square to heaven under its tented foliage. Some were planted, each on its own terrace no larger than a bed; some, trusting in their roots, found strength to grow and prosper and be straight and large upon the rapid slopes of the valley; others, where there was a margin to the river, stood marshalled in a line and mighty like cedars of Lebanon. Yet even where they grew most thickly they were not to be thought of as a

wood, but as a herd of stalwart individuals; and the dome of each tree stood forth separate and large, and as it were a little hill, from among the domes of its companions. They gave forth a faint sweet perfume which pervaded the air of the afternoon; autumn had put tints of gold and tarnish on the green; and the sun so shone through and kindled the broad foliage that each chestnut was relieved against another, not in shadow but in light. A humble sketcher here laid down his pencil in despair.'

ROBERT LOUIS STEVENSON
Travels with a Donkey in the Cévennes

The Spanish chestnut seeds itself and grows naturally at altitudes of 500m to 1,000m on both schistose and granitic soils, but has spread in the Cévennes as a result of systematic cultivation said to have been introduced by the Benedictines in the 11th century, and was welcomed as a staple food in a region where corn is hard to grow. Tens of thousands of hectares were planted, felled, and either coppiced selectively or allowed to regenerate naturally. The nuts were either eaten fresh or preserved by drying in the *'clède'* or drying-house – small buildings in the plantations, where the harvested nuts were piled up on a grid with a slow fire burning below, and then skinned and stored. These trees were systematically cultivated for many purposes. Their new shoots provided grazing for sheep and goats in the undergrowth; the fallen leaves were gathered as litter, longer shoots were woven into baskets, the timber was used for making furniture, building, fencing, and the bark for production of tannin. Today the plantations show signs of impoverishment of the soil, and of being neither wholly wild nor properly cared for. Dead branches pile up and disease sets in – one inky fungus attacks the roots, another affects the bark and dries up the sap. In recent years, however, there seems to have been a movement to redevelop the plantations – the nuts are still gathered for food – for production of high-quality timber, or at least to maintain them for grazing, as both sheep and goats do well on the undergrowth, which compensates for the shortage of grass. And even the chestnuts overlooked by the flocks can serve to nourish the herds of wild boar, while the old trees, many of them now hollow, provide cover for many species of birds: green woodpeckers, both greater and lesser spotted woodpeckers, nuthatches, goldcrests, bullfinches, and, in summer only, pied flycatchers.

The Cévennes National Park
Essential characteristics
Protected Zone: 91,416 hectares (80% in the department of Lozère, 20% in Gard) spread over 52 communes (117 hamlets or farm dwellings, 591 inhabitants). In the Central Zone 3% is land belonging to the Park, 7% is owned by local government, 30% by the state, and 60% is private property. A legal Protection Order applies throughout.
Peripheral Zone: 237,000 hectares (50% in Lozère, 40% in Gard, 10% in Ardèche) spread over 52 communes (approximately 4,000 hamlets and 41,000 inhabitants). The Park Protection Order does not apply in the Peripheral Zone, but it benefits from a specific management programme designed to ensure promotion of the local economy, and reinforce protection projects undertaken in the Central Zone.
Altitude: The highest 1,699m (Mont Lozère), the lowest 378m (Sainte-Croix-Vallée-Française). Average altitude in the Central Zone 1,200m, average altitude of the Peripheral Zone 650m.
Geographical Regions
● Causse Méjean: calcareous plateau integral to the group of Grands Causses (Sauveterre, Méjean, Causse Noir and Larzac); average altitude 1,000m; sheep-

rearing.

- Mont Lozère: granitic massifs, highest point 1,699m, cattle-rearing, sheep-grazing.
- Montagne du Bougès: granite and schistose massif, northern slopes wooded, highest point 1,421m, cattle and sheep-rearing, forestry development.
- Valleys of the Gardons rivers, cutting through schists; La Vallée Longue (course of the Gardon d'Alès), La Vallée Français (course of the Gardon de Sainte-Croix) and La Vallée Borgne (course of the Gardon de Saint-Jean), sheep and goat-rearing, bee-keeping, chestnut plantations.
- Mont Aigoual and Lingas: schist and granite, highest point 1,565m. Pine, spruce, fir and beechwoods, forestry development, sheep and cattle-grazing.

Rivers: Atlantic side of the watershed: Lot, Tarn, Mimente, Tarnon, Dourbie, Trévezel, Jonte; Mediterranean side: the Gardons, Cèze, Hérault.

Climate: Ranges from hot with pronounced drought in summer (in the Gardons Valleys) to very cold and damp (more than 90 days frost annually) on the heights of Mont Lozère.

Fauna: Until the 19th century the density of the human population went hand in hand with a decline in the number of major wild animal species, but apart from areas of intense agricultural activity and use of chemical fertilisers, the area now covered by the National Park was serving as a refuge for a whole range of small creatures, and notably insects. Since then, the reduced amount of cultivation and the spread of heathland and forests have recreated a habitat favouring wild boar and the larger birds of prey, and smaller carnivores are also numerous. The National Park has reintroduced red deer, roe deer, beavers and griffon vultures, and is seeking to reintroduce capercailzie. The count today is 45 species of mammals, 150 of birds, 23 of reptiles and batrachians, 13 of fish.

Flora: The vegetation is very varied, as it ranges from types associated with the evergreen holm-oak, requiring a hot dry climate, to the native beech and fir combination that still flourishes on the cold wet northern slopes of Mont Lozère. In certain rocky areas there are local varieties, appearing nowhere else, perhaps 10 in all, taking the two Park zones together. The many peat-bogs, too, harbour sphagnum mosses and sundews. About 20 of the 400 species enjoying nationwide protection (martagon lilies, pheasant-eye narcissus and various orchids) are found in the Park, which can count in all some 1,200 species.

Together the two Park zones boast more than 150,000 hectares of forest. Of the 40,000 hectares in the Central Zone, half of them broad-leaved, half conifers, two-thirds consist of species native to the region, one-third of newly introduced conifers. The extensive state forest of Mont Aigoual is the fruit of reafforestation work carried out in the late 19th century. Spanish chestnuts, cultivated here for more than 1,000 years (40,000 hectares in the whole Cévenol region, of which a tenth are in the Central Zone of the Park), are a typical feature of the landscape.

Administration

The Cévennes National Park is a public institution, organised on a national basis under the oversight of the Ministry of the Environment, with its headquarters at Florac in Lozère. It is run by an Administrative Council representative of both the local population and the national interest. In the intervals between meetings of the Council, ten of its elected members constitute a permanent commission responsible for day-to-day decisions. The Administrative Council is assisted by specialist commissions on agriculture, architecture and historical sites, hunting and shooting rights, fisheries, tourism and cultural activities.

The Park Director and Assistant Director manage a staff some 60 strong, comprising both outdoor personnel – the Park wardens and section heads, and specialised services – biology, social sciences, architecture, communications, administration. Another 20 seasonal assistants complete the picture.

The Park is financed by the state, its annual expenditure currently representing 40 centimes per head of the population of France.

The Peripheral Zone benefits from a management programme approved by an inter-departmental commission of 70 members representing Lozère, Gard and Ardèche. Its finances, derived from various ministerial sources, are used in support of operations aimed at maintaining the level of population in the area, increasing the facilities available for welcoming tourists, protecting sites of historical and cultural interest, and generally improving the standard of living in the region.

Park Regulations

- Absolutely NO FIRES... the scars they cause are irreversible, the damage catastrophic.
- No camping and no caravans in the Central Zone of the Park.
- Take your rubbish away with you, it always causes pollution and sometimes serious injury.
- Do not pick or damage flowers, plants or trees, whether wild or cultivated. Respect enclosures, whether walls or fences. Shut gates behind you.
- No dogs except on a leash, they disturb both wildlife and farm animals.
- Cars and cycles MUST keep to the road or track.
- Agriculture, farming and forestry continue within the Park, which helps to finance their development. Any plans for forestry projects must be submitted to the Director for approval.
- Hunting and shooting within the Park are strictly controlled (according to game licences issued, number of days permitted, shooting programmes, restricted areas etc.). Fishing is subject to the national regulations.

THE TOUR DU MONT LOZERE

WALK 1

GR68: Introduction

A number of *Grande Randonnée* footpath routes converge and crisscross on the Mont Lozère massif. The first of them is the GR68, starting from Mont Aigoual and following the Cévennes ridges from col to col, keeping to the line of the Atlantic/Mediterranean watershed. It runs along the eastern rim of the Bougès range from Jalcreste to La Croix de Berthel, then by degrees climbs the steeps of Mont Lozère, passes through Le Pont du Tarn, the Col de Finiels and Le Bleymard, and crosses the River Lot at La Remise before attacking the ascent of the Goulet. This is the Draille du Gévaudan and the European footpath No 4.

A variant, the GR72, starting from Barre-des-Cévennes, climbs the Bougès, crosses the GR7 at Le Pont du Tarn, then runs down to Villefort by way of Le Mas de la Barque.

In the course of its wide circuit the GR68 crosses these different paths, sharing the route first of one for a while, then of the other.

The GR43, faithfully following the line of the Draille de Margeride, runs through Florac, climbs the Mont Lozère range close to its western border, passing the foot of the Echine d'Aze; then reaches the Col de la Loubière, crosses the River Lot and plunges on into the Margeride.

The GR44, coming in from the east through Les Vans and Malons, follows the GR68 from Villefort to the Croix des Faux, first along the northern face of the massif, then on its western border along with the GR43.

In these sparsely populated mountains, parts of which are virtually uninhabited, finding food and shelter is a matter of prime concern. But short detours off the GR68 do link up main centres: Le Bleymard, then Bagnols-les-Bains, and from La Fage the GR68 itself runs southward to reach Florac. And along the southern stretch there are detours to Mijavols, Champlong de Bougès near Le Pont de Montvert, and then Les Bastides close to La Croix de Berthel.

On the eastern stretch the GR72, which crosses the GR68 at the Col de la Planette, enables one to reach the Mas de la Barque, and un-waymarked footpaths run down to Génolhac and Concoules.

Difficulties

The route of the GR68 everywhere follows well-frequented tracks and footpaths, and offers no difficulty except in the case of fog on two sections: La Loubière to La Fage and Gourdouse to Les Bouzèdes.

Remember, however, that there is nowhere to obtain provisions between Florac and the Col de la Croix de Berthel except at Mijavols, farm produce, nor between La Croix de Berthel and Villefort except at Concoules, in both cases requiring a detour off the GR68.

Geological Sketch of the Lozère Massif

The road and the railway from Clermond Ferrand to Nîmes, successors of the ancient Régordane, a highway from time immemorial for the seasonal movement of livestock, as of traders and pilgrims, follow from Luc on the River Allier to Alès on the Gardon, one of the major folds of the Massif Central, the great fault which was traced by Fabre for over 70 kilometres.

To the west of this fault true mountains, reaching 1,500m altitude in the Goulet range, 1,700m in the Lozère, largely dominate the flattened eastern lip of the massif. This ancient accident corresponds with a major feature of the Hercynian structure.It forms the eastern end of the faults running in an east/west direction.Only the great fault of Orcières, forming the western limit of the Lozère block, crosses the north/south fault at the small Villefort col, at 655m the lowest pass in the whole of the Cévennes. Each block has the character of a double asymmetrically sloping roof, gentle on the south side, much steeper to the north. The Lozère range constitutes a granitic 'horst' encircled by a ring of metamorphic micaschist and gneiss, flanked on the west by small limestone *causses*, satellites of the Causse de Sauveterre.The steep Lozère escarpment rises up to the south of the long valley of the Rivers Lot and Allier, with a string of small causses:Oultet, Orcières, Le Bleymard, Pomaret along the northern edge.

The crest of the Lozère ridge is of fairly uniform height, like those of Mercoire and Le Goulet, but much broader; this 'flat top' of Lozère is a huge scarcely undulating plateau, scattered with great areas of peat.Southwards the slope is gradual.To the west, towards the Col de Montmirat, extensive Secondary outliers point to the proximity of the larger causses, the most remarkable being the long narrow saddle of the Échine d'Aze.

Finally the Bougès is a band of more or less granitised schist, shaped by erosion, and there too the cross-section shows a steep slope to the north, but a much more gradual one to the south.

H. BAULIG,
Le Plateau Central de la France

Forests of the Lozère Massif

Although its maximum altitude of 1,699m earns the Lozère only 4th place among the massifs of the Central Plateau, it has the greatest area above 1,500m – about 50 square kilometres in all.This explains the preponderance of turf and high moorland, as compared with forest.

Another characteristic of this massif is the diversity, not only of its geology, but also its climate and landscape. Rainfall at the higher levels varies from 986 millimetres at Le Bleymard to 2,482 millimetres at the Mas de la Barque.The range itself, oriented east/west, presents a north face clearly distinguishable from the south facing slopes, with altitudes ranging from 450m near Génolhac to the 1,699m of the Finiels summit. This same diversity appears in the natural vegetation ranging as follows:

Hillside level (altitude 450m-1,000m): in lower areas mainly the evergreen holm-oak, showing the penetration of Mediterranean climatic conditions along the Cévenol valleys of the Rivers Cèze and Luech;

in higher areas deciduous white and sessile oaks, associated with Spanish chestnut on the south-facing slopes, birch on the north.

Mountain level (altitude 1,000m-1,500m): in lower areas beech and fir, sometimes associated with rowan, service tree and walnut in the damper areas;

in higher and drier areas, Scots pine,

Sub-alpine level (altitude above 1,600m): covered by a short mat-grass turf, interspersed with a low-growing scrub of dwarf juniper, bilberry, heather and petty whin.

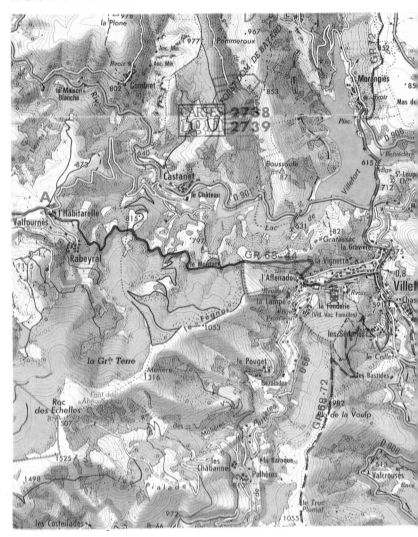

VILLEFORT

591m

Junction of the GR72, running from north to south, and the GR44, running from east to west.The GR68 and the GR44 follow the same route as far as La Croix des Faux (see map ref F).

6Km
2:00

A little beyond Le Montat there are splendid views on the right over the Altier Valley, the Villefort dam and the lake, the Château of Castanet, and the Montagne de Goulet.

L'Habitarelle
(see map ref A)
880m

Leave the northern end of Villefort by the station road on the left, and once past the station, take the road on the right across the Paillère stream. Turn right again in front of the Highways Department depot and then left on to the *'Route vieille'*. The GR68 continues along the 'old road', climbing steadily past L'Affenadou and the northern side of the valley to a small col about 750m high. Halfway up it follows the wide cart track overlooking the Altier Valley and continues westwards to the half-ruined hamlet of Le Montat.

Still following the *'Route vieille'*, marked out with granite posts, the GR winds over heathland and through spinneys, skirting several gullies of streams flowing down to the Altier. The grassy track passes below Rabeyral on the left, and over a kilometre farther on reaches the squat bell tower of L'Habitarelle.

The GR follows a tarmac road westwards from L'Habitarelle.It passes a track on the left to Valfournès and continues to Villespasses at

The 'Old Road'
Between Villefort and the Col de la Loubière the GR68 follows almost the same route as this road, known as 'old' because that is what it became after the 'route nationale' linking Villefort and Mende was built in the 1850s.

This route, certainly one of the oldest in the region, runs through a relatively soft and well populated landscape.It leaps from col to col across small ridges which are gentle enough here for it to have been built without great expense or effort. Elsewhere in the Cévennes the sharp relief and precipitous slopes are a major obstacle to the creation of new roads.

Even here, though, the route is not a particularly easy one, and in many places the path has to skirt around part of a spur or mountain shoulder, though seasoned walkers may take short cuts running straight up and over the ridge.

In the 17th and 18th centuries the road is known to have been used chiefly by muletrains carrying produce and merchandise of various sorts down to the Rhône valley and the south.Even today there are people who can remember seeing mules laden with great goatskin bottles of wine. The mail coaches, too, ventured on to this old 'royal road', stopping at the staging posts that mark out its route, like the fortified farm at La Prade, and L'Oustal Crémat (meaning the 'burnt house' in the 'Oc' or 'occitan' language, and so called because of the terracotta colour taken on by its moss covered *lauzes,* or roof-shingles, as they have weathered).

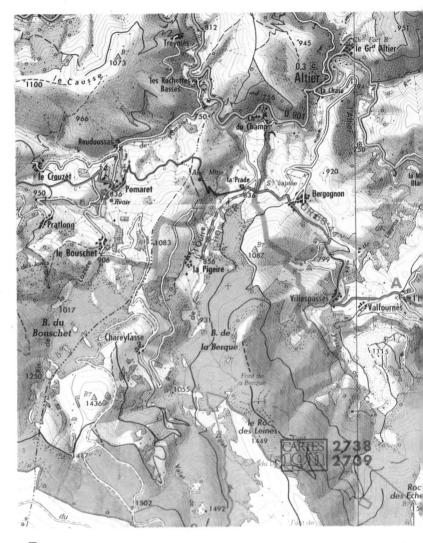

845m after crossing the Lieyros stream. Leaving the hamlet, it turns right into a chestnut plantation, then in a small valley crosses the Passadou stream at 799m, and climbs up to cut across the tarmac road again to Bergognon at 891m. The GR continues westwards by the *'Route vieille'* which climbs down steeply to the terraced valley of La Combe de Bron and to the old fortified farm, La Prade, at 836m.

Detour
LA PIGEIRE
6.5Km ⌂
1:45 856m
Take the track on the left
adjacent to La Prade.

The GR leaves the buildings on the right and goes down a pretty track to a mountain stream, La Pigeire, flowing down to the Altier, and crosses it by a small iron bridge at 801m. It goes through a small chestnut plantation and climbs up northwards in the direction of an old mine. The GR then turns to the west and through a hairpin bend with a wayside cross, reaches the hamlet of Pomaret on the right bank of a stream. Cross over the stream by a rustic footbridge to the left bank and the church by a crossroads.

POMARET
⚒
(see map ref B)
836m

5.5Km
1:30

Leave Pomaret from the church westwards by the tarmac road, going straight ahead at first and then climbing up through a series of hairpin bends. At the third bend, leave the tarmac road for the *'Route vieille'*, ignoring the Crouzet track on the right. The GR climbs south westwards over the southern slope of the schist, through heathland dotted with broom and a few copses of beech trees, rejoining the motor road 100 metres from the Col Bourbon. There is a fork 100 metres beyond the col and the GR takes the left hand track, descending to the east into a small

Forests on Mont Lozère: The Natural Woodland
The sub-alpine level is treeless, and the forests of the lower hillsides having been considerably reduced either by the axe, the extension of grazing or by fire, only the 'mountain' level is of any great interest from the forestry angle.

Pollen analyses carried out in the peat bogs of Les Sagnes above the Col des Laubies have made it possible to establish the botanical development of the forest cover, which has passed from northern birchwoods to deciduous oak, then to the less northerly beech and fir forests. From the iron age onwards human intervention has reduced the extent of the beechwoods, with a corresponding increase in heather and moorland. In our own era this evolution has continued with the elimination of the fir, which is useless as firewood, and extension of the beech forest pure and simple, more recently threatened in its turn by the extension of pastureland and the seasonal movement of stock into the mountains.

Today the most important natural forests are those on the north eastern face of the range: the forests of Longuefeuille, Les Armes, Rabeyral, La Berque, Le Bouschet. Beech predominates, but there is native pitch pine in several places, such as Le Bois des Armes, Rabeyral, La Pigeire and Servies. Still on the northern slopes there are Scots pine forests near Coursoles and the Col Bourbon, stretching westwards above the valley of the River Lot and the Valdonnez basin.

The southern slopes, on the other hand, have been subject to much more clearing and can boast only a few remaining areas of beech – ancient ecclesiastical or seigniorial holdings such as the forests of Le Mas de la Barque, Gourdouse and Le Commandeur.

gully. The track gets wider, crosses the Cubiérettes stream at 962m, and joins the road again. It crosses the terraced Comballio valley to the Altier and crosses the bridge to the village of Cubières.

The GR leaves Cubières south westwards, ignoring the road on the right along the bank of the Rieutord, and taking the left hand track which climbs up to a reservoir at 1,019m. It then follows

CUBIÈRES
⌂ ✕ ♨
(see map ref C)
989m

a pleasant track on the right, and after 600 metres, at a hairpin bend, starts on a tree lined footpath leading to Neyrac at 1,070m. Beyond Neyrac, it follows the road for 50 metres and then joins the *'Route vieille'* on the left, across a landscape of pasture land and small woods. At the first crossroads, the track begins to climb and 500 metres farther on, after having gone through a pine wood, bears west to the Col Santel, 1,195m high.It is here that the GR crosses the Draille de Gévaudan, and then the GR67 – make sure the gates are closed.

4.5Km
1:20

Detour *40 mins*
LE BLEYMARD
⌂ 🏕 🍴 🍷 🚉 🚌 🅿
1,069m
Follow the GR7 northwards for 2 kilometres.It is possible to return to the GR68 at Orcières (see map ref D) via Le Cayre.
Detour
LE CHALET DU MONT LOZÈRE
⌂
1,421m
Follow the GR7 southwards for 3 kilometres.

From the Col Santel the GR descends to the ruins at the Mazel mine, joins the D20 road, and crosses the Malavieille stream. It continues on the D20 for 250 metres northwards as far as the hamlet of Le Mazel.

LE MAZEL
⌂
1,100m

2Km
0:25

The GR leaves the D20 for a small track on the left which joins the tarmac road at a wayside cross. Beyond the col the GR leaves the road at a left hand bend and continues parallel and to the right of the road, rejoining it near the hamlet of Vareilles and going on to Orcières.

Orcières
(see map ref D)
1,072m
The track from Le Bleymard via Le Cayre joins the GR68 on the right.

The GR leaves Orcières north westwards, with a road connecting up with the D901 on the right, and crosses the bridge over the Orciérette. It continues in the direction of Le Mas d'Orcières, and 400 metres beyond, with Le Cheyroux on the right, comes to a crossroads with a fine standing stone at altitude 1,170m.

Detour
Saint-Julien-du-Tournel
Picturesque village overlooking Lot Valley.
Follow the right hand track at the crossroads to the north

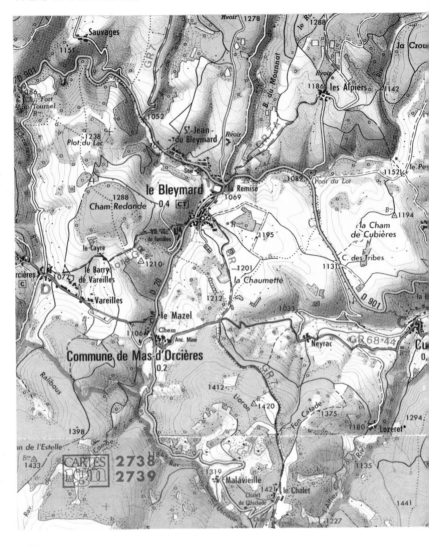

west for 3 kilometres.

4Km
1:15

Detour
BAGNOLS-LES-BAINS
🏠 🏕 🍴 🍷 ⚓ 🚂
912m

Detour see left. Follow the right hand track to Saint-Julien-du-Tournel and at the junction with the D901 road turn left to the north west for approximately 2 kilometres. It is possible to return to the GR68 at altitude mark 1,065m, east of L'Oustal Crémat (not marked on the IGN 1/50,000 map) by the D41.

The Mines at Le Mazel

From Villefort the GR68 runs along sometimes to the right and sometimes to the left of a long fault which extends as far as the Col de la Loubière. At the level of this break the schistose rock comes into contact with the limestone that stretches between Goulet and Mont Lozère, from Cubières to Mas d'Orcières, and, more closely still, between Cubières and Pomaret.

This zone has been subject to an important mineralisation of blende (zinc sulphide) and galena (lead sulphide) which were mined from very ancient times. Some of the old workings still in good condition have yielded such artefacts as bronze lamps and wedges for extracting the ore, certain of which suggest they were already in use in the Gallo-Roman period. Later, in the 17th century, it seems that Louis XIV's finance minister Colbert got in miners from Alsace to start these mines working again.

In 1892 research undertaken between Pomaret and Mas d'Orcières led to the opening of a blende and galena mine at Mazel, where most of the workings are still in good order. After two temporary closures this venture was finally shut down in 1952 despite the rich amount of mineral there. The local population suffered from the loss of jobs, but many of the miners who were also farmers have since expanded in the latter sphere, and for them the mines are no more than a fading memory.

The mining industry, which no longer seems to be regarded as a worthy occupation in the region, has been partly supplanted by the revival of agriculture and by development of high quality tourist amenities. A concrete example of this change is that some of the mine buildings are being taken over by the National Park to house an information centre and a *gîte d'étape*.

The GR, following the old mail coach road, descends into the Oultet valley and crosses the stream by an old, partly ruined, stone bridge at 980m. The track climbs steeply up towards the west, crosses through a pretty chestnut plantation and joins the Oultet to Saint-Julien-du-Tournel road at a hairpin bend.

Junction with Oultet to Saint-Julien-du-Tournel road
(see map ref E)
1,056m
Detour
OULTET
☎
Take the Oultet to Saint-Julien-du-Tournel road on the left, south eastwards for 300 metres.

From the culvert at the junction, by altitude mark 1,056m, the GR follows a gravelled track climbing up to the north west for 200 metres. At the first crossroads it turns right to the foot of La Felgère, 1,171m high, and at the second crossroads turns left, south westwards, into the forest. The GR follows the forestry road which winds down into a wide woodland glen to the road climbing up southwards towards Auriac.

Detour *20 mins*
AURIAC
🏠☎

5Km
1:30

1,186m
Storm warning bell tower.
Follow the road on the left for
1 kilometre.

At altitude mark 1,065m the GR
joins the D41 road which, on

Continue westwards. A little farther on cross the steep Pradillous valley, and a short climb then leads to the D41 road.

At the junction the GR follows the tarmac road from Le Bouchet for about 150 metres, and then

Reafforestation of Mont Lozère.

During the 18th and first part of the 19th centuries the increased need for firewood and the expansion of stockkeeping led to accelerated deforestation, bringing active erosion and ever more devastating floods in the valleys of the Tarn and Lot, as well as a progressive silting up of the Gironde estuary and the port of Bordeaux.

Laws of 1860 and 1882 relating to the restoration of mountain territories (known as 'RTM') entrusted the Forestry Service with a grandiose and inspiring mission of reconquest.It began at the end of the 19th century with conifer plantations on the Loubière which today form the magnificent full-grown and wholly 'artificial' forests of spruce on Les Laubies and pitch pine on the Mas de la Barque and Commandeur. This work of reafforestation of state-owned land continues today on the Finiels massif, where 2,000 hectares of moorland and pasture are in process of replanting, with pitch pine in the protected zone of the National Park where the climate is fairly harsh, and with fir, spruce, and beech in adjacent areas lower down.Reafforestation techniques have been evolving also, with mechanical clearing and soil preparation replacing cutting and planting by hand.But the objective remains the same: establishment of new forest with a view to halting erosion and retaining the runoff waters, while at the same time developing large areas of pastureland for the maintenance of local and transhumant stock.

This concern for maintaining a balance between the respective interests of farming and forestry has been apparent for some 30 years now in the work of the FFN (National Forestry Fund), aimed at increasing the nation's timber production whilst also endeavouring to keep the mountain farmers on their land.Reafforestation projects, many of them coupled with improvement of pastoral resources, have been achieved on sectional land in the Communes of Cubiérettes and Altier, as well as on private properties in those of Pont de Monvert, Saint-Maurice de Ventalon, Vialas etc.Taken together, these projects, whether originated by the RTM or the FFN, have restored to the slopes of Mont Lozère their ancient mantle of forest – though the woodland gracefully withdraws as one approaches the summit, whose original bare outline will always be remembered as the 'bald mountain' by lovers of this splendid Cévenol massif.

the right, leads north eastwards for 3 kilometres to Bagnols-les-Bains.

Junction

The GR68 and the GR44 join the GR43, running north and south, and all follow the same route southwards as far as the Croix des Faux (see map ref F).The GR43 to the north goes by the Draille de Margeride via Chadenet.

a grassy track on the left to L'Oustal Crémat (not marked on the IGN 1/50,000 map). It continues along a wide forest path which climbs up below a beautiful coniferous wood to the Draille de Margeride.

The GR68 continues for another 300 metres westwards to the Col de la Loubière – also known as the Col du Massequin.

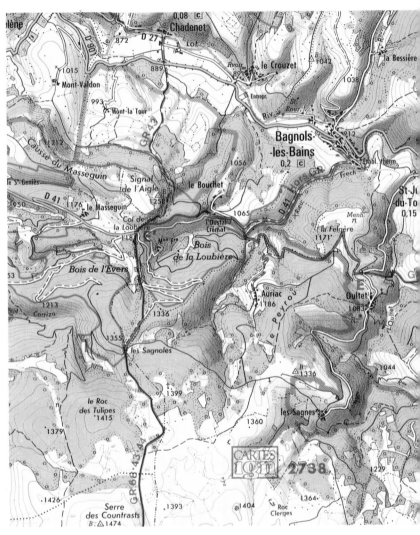

Col de la Loubière
(see map ref E)
1,181m

The GR continues on the Draille de Margeride which crosses the D41 road, and climbs a steep slope, turning to the south.It is joined by the Loubière forest path 600 metres farther on, climbing up in hairpin bends, and proceeds directly southwards, encumbered with rocks and large bushes, to the Col des Sagnoles at 1,325m.

Alternative route. It is possible to avoid the

steep ups and downs of the GR from the Col de la Loubière by taking the D41 road to the east, and then after 500 metres, the forestry road.The forestry road, after 3 hairpin bends, joins the GR on the Draille de Margeride a little before Les Sagnoles.

From the Col des Sagnoles the GR climbs a gentle slope southwards on the gravelled forestry road, and after 3 kilometres reaches a crossroads at altitude mark 1,436m.

8.5Km
2:30

One track, to the south east, goes to the Croix de Maître Vidal, another, south west to the ancient Barrandon pool, while the GR follows the track in the middle southwards over the short turf.It passes a little to the east of the Roc des Chiens Fous and through a plantation of young trees.The GR continues on the Draille de Margeride, descending gently down to the western edge of the state forest of Les Faux and crosses the road from Les Laubies to the Barrandon pool. The draille leaves the forest and keeping to the south south west, its route marked

---

Traditional Architecture

The village of La Fage is especially notable for its traditional architecture, having fine examples of the various components of rural style in the region grouped together side by side: the storm warning bell tower, the village bread oven, the cross, the covered fountain, the forge (for branding cattle).The bell tower stands beside the road, immediately noticeable for its splendid granite stonework. Many of such bell towers have disappeared, but some, like this one, remain to show what life was like in these hamlets, when winter blizzards cut them off from all outside contact, and the snow fell so thick as to obliterate every landmark and sign of direction in the whole countryside.

For centuries their bells rang out so that anyone who missed the path – people returning from market, pilgrims, or traders from the fair – could find their way by the sound, calling them back to warmth and life. The bells were used for other occasions too.Where the parish church was far away they rang out the angelus, and were also used to salute the birth of a baby, or tolled for a death of a villager.

Along the crest of the Mont Lozère range there is little but the tough mat-grass turf which for many centuries has provided summer grazing for sheep brought up from the valleys, and here we are on the route of the Draille de Margeride, that runs in a line south west/north easterly for 100 kilometres. A great mass of large granite boulders on a high ridge is known as the Roc des Chiens Fous (Mad Dogs Rock). Farther on, where a track leads off to Barrandon, is the Salt Rock, so called from the custom of using such relatively flat rocks for putting out salt for the sheep. On this rock the action of the salt has scoured and whitened the granite.

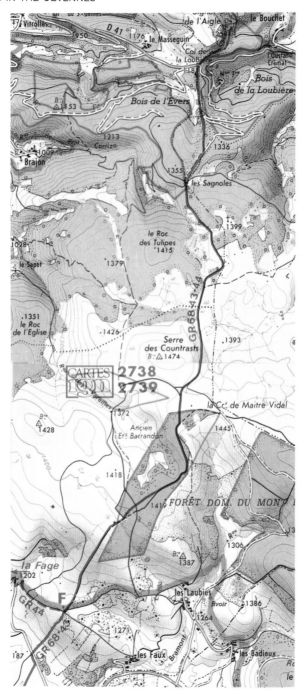

out for the migrating flocks and herds with cairns and granite blocks, reaches the Croix des Faux.

Croix des Faux
(see map ref F)
1,258m
Junction *The GR44 separates from the GR68 and GR43 on the right and goes on to La Fage and the Col de Montmirat.The GR68 and GR43 continue to follow the same route as far as Florac.*
Detour *20 mins*
LA FAGE
⌂ ☎
Follow the GR44 westwards, to the right, for 1 kilometre.
Detour *20 mins*

6Km
1:40

LES LAUBIES
⌂ ✗
Follow the path to the east for 1 kilometre.

This stretch of the Draille de Margeride provides a distant view to the south east of the line of fallen menhirs of Les Bondons, splendid views of the western end of the Lozère range to the north, and of the gorges of the river Tarn at Ispagnac to the south

The draille, its course dotted with rocks, descends to the south west for about 700 metres to the road which connects La Fage to the D35 and to Les Bondons.It becomes no more than a track alongside the road for 200 to 300 metres to the south east, and then turns to the south west again, to the ford across the Bramont stream. The draille climbs up the gully from the stream to cross the D35 and, wide again, continues straight ahead.It is then waymarked with cairns as a guide for the transhumance, and descends for about 1.5 kilometres towards the hamlet of Les Combettes.

Pass through Les Combettes, and after crossing over the culvert of the Brenou stream join the draille again on the left where Les Combes track branches off.The draille at first climbs steeply to the south east, then to the south, and crosses through the state forest of Les Gorges du Tarn to the foot of the Échine d'Aze, a *causse* or small limestone plateau.

Legends of Mont Lozère and Le Bougès

Two rounded knolls dominate Les Bondons, their steep bare slopes of blue marl and limestone rising more than 300 metres above the desolate countryside. These are the *'puechs'*, or pikes of Les Bondons and of L'Échine (or Esquino) d'Aze, the neighbouring limestone ridge.

The origin of these twin *puechs* puzzled past generations, and knowing nothing of science or geology they looked to mythology for an explanation, attributing them to the friendly giant Gargantua – the Hercules of the Gauls.

After a day's work on the nearby *causse,* they said, Gargantua was on the way back to his home somewhere in the Cévennes. He was wearing sabots (the gods were made in the image of man), and the sabots were very heavy with the mud of the field he had been working in. After crossing the steep ridge of the Échine d'Aze, to make walking easier he sat down and scraped the mud off his sabots. Then he piled up the scrapings to form these two *puechs* – which is why they look so alike.

The Menhirs of Les Bondons

At the Bramont ford the route passes from the granite of the Lozère range to the limestone of the Cham des Bondons. Climbing up southwards across the plateau you will come upon fallen granite monoliths. These are menhirs, some of great size, 3 to 6 metres long, and are generally situated on the highest parts of the bare stony saddle characteristic of the region. These megalithic monuments, most of them spindle-shaped, originally stood upright, their smoothly rounded tops and angles indicating fairly well developed workmanship.

west.There is a good water point at the hamlet of Les Combettes, once a relay station for the mail coaches on the old Mende to Florac road.

Echine d'Aze

(see map ref G)

1,233m

At La Maison Neuve, a small abandoned farmhouse, a pool of running water by the side of the track shows that you have left the zone of porous limestone for a zone of impermeable granite.The transition shows up in the blue grey colour of the marl.
Lower down, to the west, you will find Issenges farm, also virtually abandoned, noteworthy for its architecture hewn out of the limestone.Leaving the limestone again, the draille makes contact with the marls once more, going down towards the Tarn valley.Cut into the cliffs, it crosses through chestnut woods, an indication of the presence of schist.

9Km
2:45

Pont de la Bessède

(see map ref H)

546m

The GR68 and GR43 separate, the GR43 continuing southwards.

Detour

FLORAC

⌂ ⌂ 𝐀 ✕ ϒ ⚏ ▭ 🛈

546m

Situated at the foot of the Méjan causse; old castle; Headquarters of the Cévennes National Park.
Follow the GR43 southwards for approximately 800 metres. At the Pont de la Bessède north of Florac the path climbs

From the ridge at the foot of the *causse* the GR68, following the draille, descends gradually down, southwards, to La Maison Neuve with its spring at 961m by the track to Mont-Méjan on the right.It continues to descend for another 2 kilometres to the track leading up to the fortified farm of Issenges, and less than 2 kilometres more to the south, reaches the zone of the coniferous forest.The draille continues into the forest, while the GR follows the hairpin bends on the left down through the chestnut plantation, and after 1,500 metres reaches the family holiday village.It joins the N107 road and crosses the Pont du Tarn at 543m, continuing on the N106 for approximately 500 metres to the Pont de la Bessède.

At the bridge over the Tarnon take the path climbing up behind the retaining wall and follow it as far as a meadow planted with apple trees.Where the path becomes a gravelled track, at the far end of the meadow, take the narrow track on the right in the thicket and climb up among the chestnut trees for about 500 metres to the south east.Coming out of the wood continue up over the hillside along by a low wall, and after 300 metres follow the upper path which climbs towards a ruined open cow byre. The path sweeps round to the north, skirts the southern slope of the Montagne de Lempézou, and passing by an ancient spring marked by a willow tree it reaches a shelf overlooked by a cherry tree.

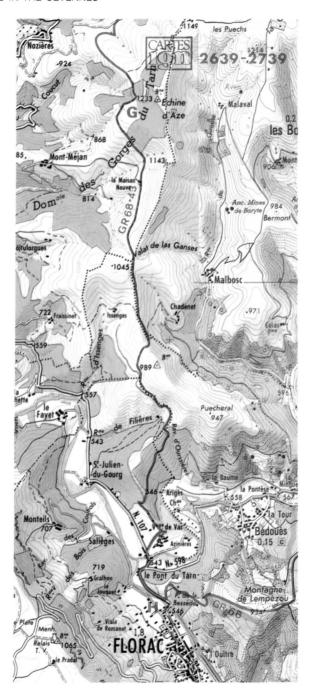

steeply over the schist, through a plantation of chestnuts overgrown with broom. Take notice of the small terraces below, witnesses of a past age. Here and there it is easy to imagine the land put to growing cereals, where today the oak has established itself.

5Km
2:00

From the point where it leaves the chestnut wood up to the Col de la Chaumette the track is on limestone, and the villages of Bédouès and Cocurès are in view down in the Tarn valley. While crossing the ridge, where the track changes direction from the east to the west slope of La Chaumette, observe the schist below, shown by the appearance there of chestnuts, and so down to the bottom of the valley.

The GR then enters a coniferous forest, passing 2 ruined open cow byres, and leading up to the Col de Lempézou at 891m. The track turns to the north skirting the western slope of La Chaumette, and then to the south east to skirt the eastern slope. It joins up with the forestry road of La Chaumette coming up from La Pontèse on the N598 road via Bédouès, and continues in a general direction eastwards towards the Col du Sapet.

La Chaumette Forestry Road

(see map ref I)
At the Col de Perpau the limestone ends and we are again on the schist, home of the Corsican Laricio pine which flourishes best on siliceous soils. This stretch of the GR runs along south facing slopes, with views away to the heights of the Can de Ferrières, the Can de Tardonnenche, and even farther south to the Can de l'Hospitalet. After passing the Col de l'Encize the path switches to the opposite slope, where again there are outcrops of schist. Beyond the Ramponenche state forest it finally reaches the high pastures, domain of the sheep, with heathery moorland and

7Km
2:00

The GR68 follows the wide forestry road which makes its way eastwards through many twists and turns, crosses through a coniferous wood, and on to the foot of a large reservoir. Farther on the GR reaches a large clearing with a cottage at the entrance providing shelter – on leaving the clearing notice the 2 tall conifers blasted by lightning. At the junction with the cart track descending to the north the GR goes to the right, and a little farther on crosses the Col de Perpau (sometimes known as the Col du Fraysse) at 952m.

Continuing past a track descending southward to the Bergerie de Perpau the GR goes on to the southern slope of the Montagne de Ramponenche, crossing over to the northern slope at the Col de l'Encize at 1,026m. After a stretch through the forest it emerges at another col at 1,056m where a little track descends steeply down towards the D20 road southwards. To the north another track goes to the Mines of Ramponenche where there are splendid views over the valleys of the Tarn and

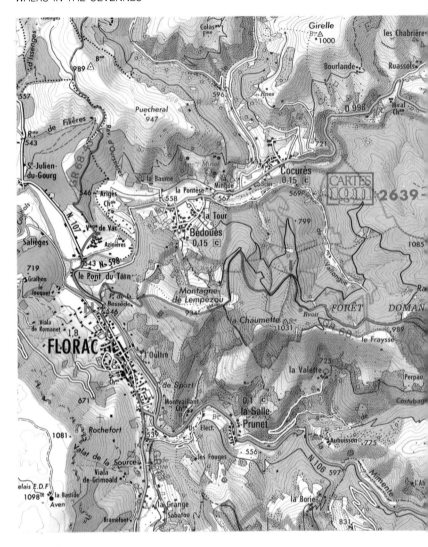

scattered stands of beech. This landscape is particularly attractive in autumn, with extensive views over the southern slopes of Mont Lozère, where hamlets and villages lie in a chain from west to east, sheltered from cold north winds by the massif itself.

the Mimente. Following the northern slope of Le Sapet, 1,116m high, the GR reaches the Col du Sapet.

Col du Sapet

(see map ref J)

1,080m

The D20 road from Saint-Julien-d'Arpaon to Le Pont de Montvert crosses the GR68 at the col.

Detour *20 mins*

MIJAVOLS

⌂

925m

At the junction with the D20 road take the track on the right descending eastwards down the southern slope for 2 kilometres.

Detour

LE PONT DE MONTVERT

Ⓗ ⌂ ⋀ ✗ ⵑ ⛴ ▬ 🅑

Follow the D20 road to the north for 4 kilometres

The GR crosses the Bougès massif along the line of the crest from west to east at an altitude ranging from 1,200 to 1,400m. The northern slope is the realm of the beech (the Bois d'Altefage); to the south heathery moorland predominates, pasturage for sheep. Micaschist prevails for the whole of this stretch, easily recognisable by its flaky and glistening appearance, due to the amount of mica in it. From the 1,421m altitude mark shown on the map you can see the whole of the Mont Lozère range, from the ancient Barrandon pool in the west as far as the Cassini summit in the east.

The GR72 coming up from Barre des Cévennes north eastwards to Villefort crosses the GR68 at the Col de la Planette.

7.5Km
2:10

The GR continues across the side of the mountain to the southern slope along a very old track occasionally covered with heather. After 700 metres it crosses a little ridge to the northern slope where it threads its way through a small beech grove. The track then climbs up to a grassy ridge from where the Signal du Bougès, 1,421m high, can be seen straight ahead, crowned with a large cairn. The GR goes along this ridge, then skirts the summit to the north and passes by the cairn approximately 100 metres away.

A wide firebreak through an extensive conifer afforestation leads up to a small summit with a boundary post on it. The GR descends by the side of an enclosure to the Col de la Planette, 1,200 metres farther on to the east.

A kilometre still farther to the east, at altitude mark 1,362m, the track reaches the Col du Bougès.

Col du Bougès

(see map ref K)
1,308m
*Monument; the 'route
Pomaret' from Pont de
Montvert and 'Quatre
chemins' to the Col de
Jalcreste, skirting the upper
basin of the Mimente,
crosses the GR68.*

The GR follows the ridge eastwards past altitude marks 1,351m and 1,336m, a route providing extensive views to the north. It continues eastwards along a forest track, still on the ridge, past altitude marks 1,294m and 1,282m. The forest track narrows into a goat track through the heather up to the Signal de Ventalon, 1,350m high, an exceptional beauty spot.

Local History
Close to the 1,421m altitude mark between the Cols du Sapet and de la Planette, beyond the firebreak, on some of the slabs of schist there are small cavities or cups which were cut in the rock by people of very early times. Experts disagree about their purpose, but they show there must once have been pastoral activity in this region. On this stretch the footpath runs through a state forest consisting mainly of pitch pine, especially useful as providing protective cover against a rigorous climate, for new plantings of spruce and fir. This forest is about a century old.

It was in this area that the plot to assassinate the Abbé de Chayla on 24 July 1702 at Le Pont de Montvert was hatched. He had imprisoned a group of young Protestants, whom he was made to set free at the cost of his life. Esprit Séguier was the chief instigator of this struggle, supported by a few friends: Jean Couderc, Nicolas Joini, Laporte de Branoux, as well as Abraham Mazel who recorded what took place. The assassination and the subsequent disturbance triggered the outbreak of the Camisard War.

The GR7 from the Col de Jalcreste joins the GR68 at Le Ventalon and they continue on the same route as far as L'Aubaret.

5.5Km
1:15

After the Ventalon summit, and as far as L'Aubaret we are on the Draille du Gévaudan (or du Languedoc) which was used by flocks on their way from Provence and Gard to pastures on Mont Lozère, the Montagne du Goulet and Haut Gévaudan. This draille, which here and there becomes merged into forestry roads, is still used for transhumance of some 10,000 sheep in the Hôpital, Aubaret and Gourdouse areas.

The GR turns to the north and descending a short, sharp slope joins the Draille du Gévaudan, which continues for 1.5 kilometres down to the D35, and some metres farther on, the Col de la Croix de Berthel.

Col de la Croix de Berthel
(see map ref L)
1,088m
Situated on Atlantic/Mediterranean watershed; N598 crosses GR.

The GR continues, with the draille, on a forestry track climbing northwards in the Rouvières forest. At the Plo de la Nassette, at 1,151m, the draille becomes some 20 metres wide and climbs more steeply to the north north east towards the Plo de l'Estrade at 1,233m.

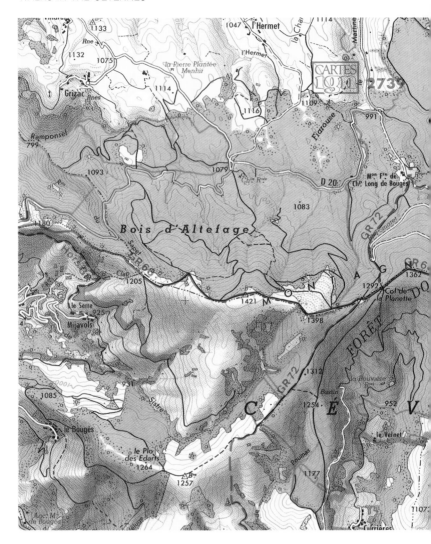

Detour
LES BASTIDES

⌂

*Follow the N598 road
northwards.*

*Extensive views to the east
over Les Tourrières,
Gourdouse, La Vialasse and
Pierre Froide; to the north,*

The draille, now narrower and here and there
paved with stones, descends steeply
northwards. It crosses the Alignon stream by
an old bridge and reaches L'Aubaret.

A 'captured' stream

Compare the course of a stream running westwards just in front l'Aubaret to the Alignon and Tarn, with that of another coming from the east, which suddenly turns back on itself and plunges southwards to the Luech and Cèze. This is a splendid example of 'capture': a relatively sluggish stream draining to the Atlantic literally 'taken over' as a result of regressive erosion, to become a fast-flowing stream running down to the Mediterranean. Notice the change in its lengthwise profile: gentle slope and broad valley, as against steep gorges, and the sharp acute-angled 'elbow' bend – and note too the name of this stream: 'Rieutort' or 'Twisted River'.

Le Croix de Berthel

6Km
1:50

the draille at L'Aubaret and the foothills of Mont Lozère.

The GR7 separates from the GR68 and follows the Draille du Gévaudan towards L'Hôpital.
From mid-June to mid-September the park at L'Aubaret, a restored fortified

The GR68 turns to the east and follows a road which crosses the Valat de la Latte – a steep terraced valley – goes through La Vialasse, at 1,300m, crosses the Valat de la Sugue, at 1,267m, to the little hamlet of Pierre Froide.

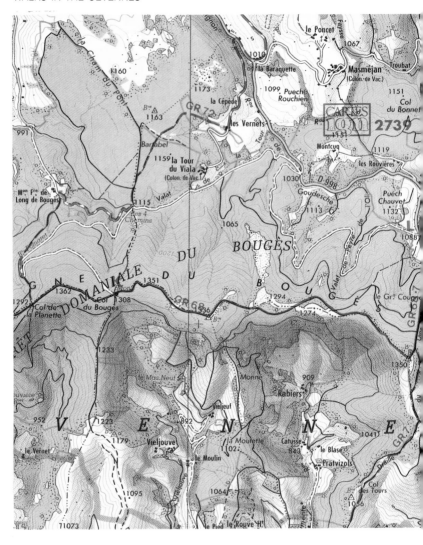

farm, is the stopping place for transhumant flocks.
Around La Vialasse you may observe kestrels perched on electric power lines, harriers with their swooping flight, and also perhaps catch sight of 'whiterumps'or wheatears. Nearer to Gourdouse buzzards are usually plentiful.

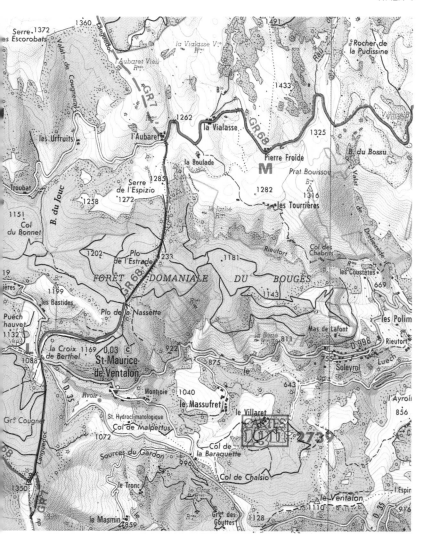

Pierre Froide
(see map ref M)
1,281m

The GR leaves the hamlet along the right bank of the Pudissine stream and after crossing a bridge to the opposite bank continues northwards to altitude 1,354m where it turns to the south east. The GR follows the Pontil stream to a partly tarred road and continues north eastwards to Gourdouse at 1,238m.

Gourdouse
1,238m

The GR skirts the southern slope, crossing the Gourdouse stream after 700 metres to the

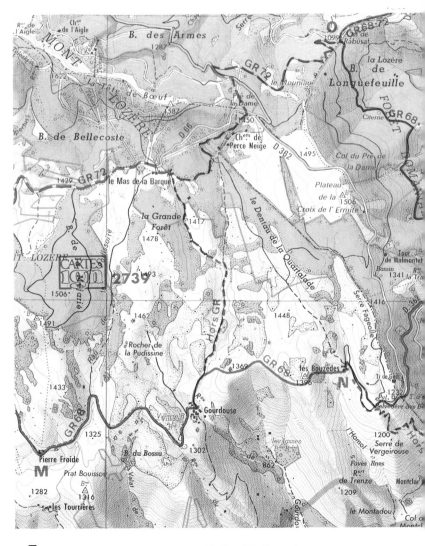

Partly in ruins, is abandoned in the winter and is not reoccupied until the snow thaws.

Numerous mini peat bogs or 'narses', where sphagnum and sundews grow, are scattered here and there on the Farou plateau, some of them 'hanging' along its

1,369m altitude mark.

Gourdouse

From the 11th century on, there was a priory here, attached to Saint-Nicolas de Campagnac, with vast estates under its care. Deserted now, we can guess what it was like in the Middle Ages, with every acre of cultivable land lovingly tilled and crisscrossed with 'béals' – the irrigation channels.

The more open, but drier, areas were given over to rye, or sometimes oats or turnips, the remainder divided between pasture, stands of beech, and farther north the great forest, haunt of roe deer, wild boar – perhaps even bears. Thus in the 14th century we find the Prior of Gourdouse receiving an edict regulating the amount of timber to be cut, the hunting, the maintenance of pastures, use of water, and steps to be taken to prevent pollution of streams. Proper manuring of fields was assured by the flocks who grazed here – and was systematically organised. According to the amount of land he owned, each peasant had the right to so many 'nights' – or parts of nights – of manure from the visiting flocks that came each summer to graze.

Overpopulated in the 19th century, this village inhabited by peasants who worked in the Vialasse silver mines was destroyed by fire, and then what was left was pulled down in the 20th century. Nothing remains of the old hamlet except the house of M.Pellecuer, the last inhabitant, and a few ruins.

---

edge. Typical of Cévenol streams is the Homol, slow-flowing through a broad, rounded valley at plateau level, then plunging suddenly down a precipitous gorge towards the Mediterranean. Short-toed eagles frequent this area.

7.5Km
2:10

Detour
VIALAS

Follow the unwaymarked path which descends in hairpin bends southwards for 3 kilometres.

Detour
LE MAS DE LA BARQUE

Follow the path along the right bank of the Gourdouse stream northwards for 3 kilometres to the GR72.

After fording the stream the path climbs very steeply through the rocks to a pass between the 1,369m and the 1,396m altitude marks eastward as far as Les Bouzèdes (see map ref N.) Beyond the hamlet the GR crosses the Homol Stream, and on the right takes the old track bordered with blocks of granite southwards.

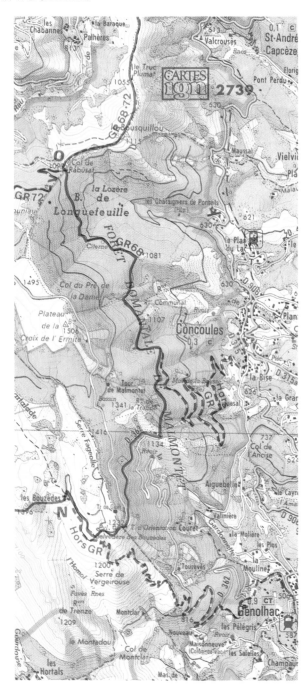

Detour *1hr 30 mins*
GÉNOLHAC

Detour see left. 500 metres beyond Les Bouzèdes a path, waymarked in red, tumbles down for 5 kilometres to Génolhac. It is possible to return to the GR68 at Le Truc du Plo, 1,134m, by the *'sentier bleu'*. The path climbs up the valley of the Gardonette stream for 3 kilometres, via La Mouline Haute and Valinière.

The GR skirts a rocky spur and reaches the Belvédère des Bouzèdes at altitude mark 1,232m.

Belvédère des Bouzèdes
1,232m
Orientation table

Entering the Malmontet forest, the GR68 follows the D362 road for about 1.5 kilometres to the first hairpin bend at a place called Le Truc du Plo, 1,134m.

The path called 'le sentier bleu' coming up the Gardonnette valley from Génolhac via Valinière joins the GR68.

The GR continues northwards along a recently constructed gravelled road where, on the left, the wooded slope is overhung by the Rocher de la Trappe. Farther north, at a hairpin bend by the 1,047m altitude mark, a forestry track leaves the GR on the right.

6.5Km
1:50

Detour *1hr 50 mins*
CONCOULES

Detour see left. The forestry track descends in a series of hairpin bends, passing the ruined Mas de la Baysse, to the ancient Régordane

---

Viewpoint at Les Bouzèdes

With its particularly well-made orientation table this is worth a stop. Besides the remarkably beautiful countryside, and without counting the more distant landmarks of the Rhône Valley and Alps, which are not always visible, you may note the following points of interest:

– The line of cols which mark out the route of the ancient Gallo-Roman highway, the 'Régordane', its alignment resulting from an important fault which also determines the steep eastern limit of the Lozère range, between Villefort and Génolhac.

– Génolhac itself, which owes its position to the fault, enjoying water, a pass, cultivable land and tile clay.

– Beyond the River Cèze the Aujac plateau, a 'hidden *causse*' with its hamlets all in a line along a fault which brings them water.

– The east/west orientation of the several Gardons river valleys and the steep *serres* or ridges which separate them, making communications in the Cévennes especially difficult.

Finally there is the close proximity of the Mediterranean, which explains how the intense erosion in this area has come about, erosion still further accentuated by the very high annual rainfall – nearly 2 metres – in Lozère.

640m

highway leading to Concoules – a total of 6 kilometres. A path, which is not shown on the map, descends directly down to the village, 2 kilometres from the junction of the GR and the forestry track.

The GR winds through the forest and at altitude mark 1,081m passes the Col du Marquet, a curious rocky mass on the right.

The GR continues northwards passing a large reservoir and reaches, at altitude mark 1,071m, a hairpin bend of the Bois de Longuefeuille forestry road which leads, 1.5 kilometres farther on, to the Col de Rabusat.

Col de Rabusat

(see map ref O)
1,099m
The GR72 joins the GR68 from Le Mas de la Barque and follows the same route to Villefort by the long crest with its 3 peaks, Le Bousquillou, 1,115m, Le Truc Plumat, 1,055m and Le Plo de la Voulp, 982m.

8Km
2:15

From the col the GR is clearly marked and follows a low stone wall indicating the boundary between the Gard and the Lozère departments. But soon the track, more or less overgrown with broom, is less clearly defined, and leaves the crest on the left for the western slope. It joins the crest again towards Le Truc Plumat and follows it to Le Plo de la Voulp, becoming well defined once more going through a wood on the eastern slope.

Warning Be careful not to miss the forestry track on the right, as its start is not clearly indicated on the IGN 1/50,000 map.

The GR follows the forestry track through several hairpin bends on the eastern slope to Les Sédariès farm where camping is provided for. From there a new road serving a housing estate joins the N106 above the railway bridge close to Villefort.

VILLEFORT

(see map ref P)
591m
Villefort takes its name from the Château de Montfort standing above Villefort's 'collet' or knoll – one among the series of 'Mont' castles encircling Mont Lozère, such as Montmirat, Montvert, Montcuq, Montjoie, etc.

TOUR EN PAYS CÉVENOL:

THE GARDONS VALLEYS: WALK 2

GR67: Introduction

The joys of walking and exploration go hand in hand for people attracted to the Cévennes, these magical mountains where man has shaped the landscape and become one with it: a landscape of schist and limestone revealed in all its beauty and human interest by the GR67 footpath waymarked by the Comité National des Sentiers de Grande Randonnée.

Exploring the Cévennes on foot is a matter of tradition. R.L. Stevenson in his long peregrination across the Massif Central was aiming for Le Pont de Montvert, Florac and Saint-Jean-du-Gard; so present-day walkers tread in the footsteps of one who trod this way before them - and who, according to some people, invented the sleeping-bag! The GR67 largely follows, first, the line of the Draille de Margeride, then the watershed between Aire-de-Côte and the Col de Jalcreste, and finally the Draille du Languedoc down to Anduze again. The route is rich in beauty-spots, in places and things of interest to visit, and is permeated with the long history of this high country: the *maison-refuge* at Aire-de-Côte, the *gîte* and rocky plateau of the Can de l'Hospitalet, the old streets of Barre-des-Cévennes, the memorial at Fontmort, the views and landscape at the Col de Jalcreste, the traverse across the ridges of La Vieille Morte, the Maison de Roland at Mas Soubeyran, and finally Anduze itself, the ancient gateway to the Cévennes.

Walkers who undertake this 'grand circular tour' of the Gardons region of the Cévennes will come to appreciate the colourful diversity of the Cévenol Serres, the ridges, plateaux and rocky crests, the forest tracks, and the old highways built by the Intendant de Bâville. A link-road between the granite bastions of Lozère and the limestone Garrigues of Gard to the south, this is a walkers' route, but also the route of the great transhumance, which happily is being revived again.

We hope that our friends the walkers who make this long trek will not forget the people who live here, whose hospitality they will enjoy, and also - if they know how to listen - whose sagacity and learning they will appreciate. At dusk, at some corner of a field or roadside halt, you have only to start the shepherds and the country people talking, to discover that they have all the wit and wisdom of the world.

Then, back at Anduze where you started from, you will surely be telling everyone about the majestic beauty of these mountains and the courage of the people who live among them. By doing so you will be true friends of the National Park, whose chief aim is the support and conservation of the Hautes Cévennes and the life of the Cévenol people.

E. LEYNAUD
Director of the Cévennes National Park 1974-1978

Difficulties

The route of the GR67 is unlikely to present any difficulty on account of bad weather except between Jalcreste and Le Pereyret, on the Montagne de la Vieille Morte. At such times walkers are advised to skirt around La Vieille Morte by the GR67B.

Note also that there is no possibility of obtaining provisions between Colognac and Barre-des-Cévennes except at Les Plantiers on the GR6A.

Most of this route lies within the Cévennes National Park, and is subject to the Park regulations.

Farms of the Gardons Valleys

The farm as a whole constitutes a production unit which reflects the semi-autonomous nature of traditional peasant life here. Alongside the farmhouse itself a whole series of buildings are erected as need arises: sheepfold, pigsty (la soue), granary, storehouse, bakehouse, oast or drying-house (la clède), winepress, magnanerie (for silkworms) – all of them tucked so closely against the hillside that what is the second floor at the front or façade of the building is often the ground floor level at the back.

Planted half-way up the mountain slopes, the houses are mostly tall and sombre-looking: windows are small and the building material dark in colour. From stone-flagged entry to rooftop all is of schist, except for a few coloured pebbles from the river or pieces of mica that bring a lighter note to the walls, or perhaps to the door and window frames where these are of limestone.

Not much decoration goes into this workaday architecture. The occasional rounded arch of stone blocks set on a lintel will rise like a sun above a doorway, or little triangular niches over the windows, but these are chiefly intended to spread the weight of the wall above to either side of the opening. Chimneys alone are given any aesthetic consideration, being crowned with 'lauzes', stone shingles forming a triangle, apex uppermost, with another lauze flat on top, held in place by a heavy stone, and often adorned by a growth of moss. But you need to see these gloomy walls gleaming with silver and orange reflections after a spring shower, to understand just how all this austerity can be brightened by the green of trellised vines and the colour of flowers.

The layout of the surrounding farmland is carefully planned and organised. Water piped from a spring, sometimes along a runnel cut in the rock, is retained in tanks or cisterns and redistributed through a network of irrigation ditches. Vegetable gardens occupy terraces close to the house, with its trellis of vines, where the heat which the stone walls absorb by day radiates back to the vines at night. Farther off are the irrigated meadows, orchards, mulberry trees, and beehives made from a section of chestnut trunk with a lauze for a lid.

A solitary cypress or pine often marks the site of a small family graveyard, dating from the time when Protestants were not allowed to bury their dead in the Catholic parish cemeteries, and still in use today. Chestnut plantations encircle fields and garden: at one time these would have sheltered a few fields of rye or potatoes, and in many cases may still be grazed by sheep. And so long as bare rock does not start immediately above the farm, there would be an area of moorland, providing summer pasture for the ewes, where makeshift folds, known as 'jasses' were put up to shelter them.

These different parts of the farmland were linked by narrow tracks that were often gravelled but rarely intended for wheeled carts. Loads of produce or goods were carried on mule-back – or, more often, on the backs of men and women, and access from one terrace to the next was by steps built into the stone walls or cut in the rock.

Silkworm Breeding

Sericulture, or silkworm breeding, was carried on at Anduze at the end of the 13th century, but only spread in the mountains 400 or 500 years later. It was then that the mulberry, 'tree of gold', flourished in every valley, and in the farmhouses rooms were set

aside as cocooneries. After buying the eggs, each housewife would set them to hatch in an incubator, or in a little bag which she carried about her person. Next, the caterpillars or 'worms' were laid out on trays, and then began the daily chore of picking fresh mulberry leaves to feed the increasingly voracious larvae. Following that, branches of heather had to be cut, on which, after 4 more metamorphoses, the caterpillars would climb to spin their cocoons. Finally the cocoons were boiled in great copper basins to kill the chrysalis. Sometimes the farmers' wives themselves would empty the cocoons and spin the silk; but more often the 'harvest' was sold to the spinning mill - every village had one, where the young women and girls worked in the winter, and made quite a bit of money at it.

Pebrine, a silkworm disease which raged from 1847-68, competition from oriental silks with the opening of the Suez Canal, and the slump in cotton at the end of the century, led to the gradual disappearance of village spinning mills and of silkworm breeding as a home industry. The process was irreversible, and the last mills in the Vallée Française closed down in 1957.

Quite recently, however, experiments have been tried which seem to prove that sericulture might once again become a profitable enterprise in the Cévennes, where it once brought riches.

PH. JOUTARD AND J.N. PELEN

Geological Sketch

The dislocation of the Tertiary period broke the eastern edges of France's Massif Central into a series of raised blocks running from east to west: in the north, the Lozère range, flanked by the Goulet and Bougès heights; in the south, the Aigoual, with the Suquet and Lingas beyond it.

Strictly speaking, the Cévennes consist of these two main massifs, with a lower-lying region stretching between them. To the west of the watershed there remain extensive traces of Secondary rocks, forming the small *causses* around Barre, the most important of which is the Can de l'Hospitalet. The number and the extent of these fragments testify to the early continuity of the Secondary cover. The post-Hercynian bed which underlies them extends eastward in a series of horizontal ridges as far as the Plan de Fontmort and Mont Mars.

The river-system of the Gardons runs down from the highest point of the Cévennes in the shape of a fan, with rectilinear sections indicating the presence of ancient faults. The weak resistance offered by the schist has resulted here in its almost total breakdown; so that between the broad rocky river beds, swept by formidable autumn spates, and the narrow ridges of the Serres, long banks of broken scree develop. There are neither plateaux nor gorges, just these deep stony corridors.

Of the old post-Hercynian beds almost nothing remains: the whole region is completely broken up.

H. BAULIG

Village in Cévenol

WALK 2

ANDUZE

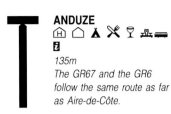

135m
The GR67 and the GR6
follow the same route as far
as Aire-de-Côte.

From the crossroads in the centre of Anduze take the D133 road westwards leading to Saint-Félix-de-Pallières. Leave this road 100 metres beyond the town, and take a tarmac road on the right called 'des Pierres Onches', which climbs gently to the south west as far as the district of Le Poulvarel, passing by the north

Anduze: Gateway to the Cévennes

Admirably situated at the foot of the Cévennes, this ancient city, gateway to the Corniche des Cévennes, the Causses and the gorges of the Tarn, bygone Roman Anduzia - *'En Deux'* that is 'in two parts', divided by the Gardon - was already providing human shelter in its limestone caves in prehistoric times.

Later, the wealthy Gallo-Romans of Nîmes, having a fondness for the rivers of the Gardon, were building second homes there, roman villas, often surrounded by large agricultural estates.

As early as the 10th century, the House of the Bernards d'Anduze, always closely allied to the Bermonds de Sauve, was one of the most powerful seigniories of the Languedoc. The Monastery of Tornac, founded by Charlemagne, bore witness to importance of the House even from the 9th century.

In the Middle Ages, the population of 6,000 enclosed within the ramparts - only the clock-tower, built in 1320, remains - made it the principal town of the foothills by their craftsmanship and commercial prowess.

Its wealth came from the introduction of the silkworm, brought from the East by the Crusades and developed later thanks to the Duke of Sully, Minister to Henry of Navarre. No fewer than 32 silk mills were scattered throughout the valley. The town's markets and fairs - see the covered market place with its pagoda fountain of glazed tiles - made it an important trading place between the Cévennes, providing wool, silk, sheep and chestnuts, and the plain, providing wine and cereals.

In the 16th century clergy and monks from the Franciscan monastery, carried the population with them into the Reformation, making Anduze 'the Geneva of the Cévennes' and the focus of the religious war of Languedoc for two centuries. When Anduze was a stronghold of the Duke de Rohan, Richelieu signed the Peace of Alais in 1629 and ordered the fortifications to be razed. The town was destined to remain at the centre of resistance at the time of the war of the Camisards, 1702-04.

A century later, the rise of the Alès coalfield hastened a decline due to a recession in the silk industry as much as a demographic and economic decline of the hinterland.

Today, the town, a residential and tourist centre, provides several campsites outside the town along the banks of the Gardon with interesting tourist attractions in the neighbourhood, such as the bamboo forest at Prafrance, the Musée du Desert and the Grottos at Trabuc.

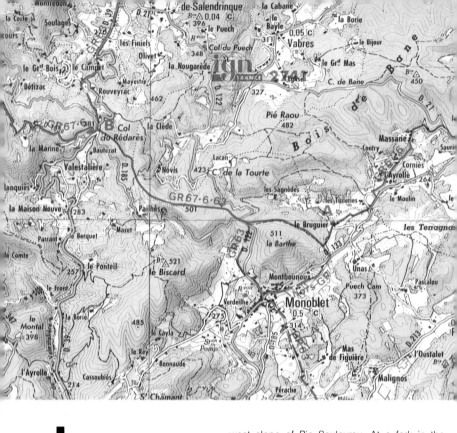

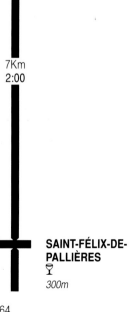

west slope of Pic Souleyrou. At a fork in the road ignore the right-hand branch, and continue straight on for several metres. Bear left at a clump of pine trees on to an old and little frequented track which climbs steeply to the south east to reach, in a residential area, a road descending to the south east. At this point take the old track in front of the electricity transformer, and rejoin the D133 a little to the east of the Col de Traviargues. Follow the D133 for about 600 metres, and at the 278m altitude mark, take the track on the left going down to La Tuilerie and Cabridiès. Cross over a stream running through a culvert, then climb up again by a path winding through groves of holm-oaks to rejoin the D133 at La Baraque. From there the road leads to Saint-Félix-de-Pallières.

SAINT-FÉLIX-DE-PALLIÈRES

300m

The GR67 follows the D133 road south west from the village. After Le Temple, at the crossroads with the D21, the GR climbs to the right along the D21, then takes a short cut to

3.5Km
1:00

Le Brugier Farm
(see map ref A)
335m

Detour 20 mins
MONOBLET
✗ ☂ ⚖
320m
At Monoblet you will
encounter waymarking of the
GR63 which, to the south, :
leads to the Pont d'Avignon,
and northwards joins the
GR67 and GR6 north of the
Barthe hill.

1.5Km
0:30

Junction with the GR63
The GR63 from Monoblet
joins the GR67 and GR6 and
then follows the same route
as far as the Col du
Rédarès.

3Km
1:00

Col du Rédarès
(see map ref B)
381m
The GR63 separates from the
GR67 and GR6 northwards.

the left to cross the first ravine and joins the
D21 again. After several metres, at the first
crossroads, the GR follows a tarmac road on
the left to Massane and continues, rejoining the
D133 to Les Tuileries close to a bridge called
Le Pont de Ribout. Cross this bridge and soon
afterwards leave the road to follow a track on
the right leading to the Brugier farm – and be
careful of the dogs.

From the farm follow a footpath skirting a wood
for 200 metres to a track on the left.

Detour see left. Follow the track to the south
east, cutting across the D133 road, and turn
right on to an old country lane from Anduze to
Monoblet. It is possible to return to the GR67
north of the Barthe hill by following the GR63
northwards.

Beyond the track on the left to Monoblet the
GR turns sharply right into a wood and bears
westward following the northern slope of the
Barthe. It rejoins the D122 at the junction with
the GR63.

The GR67 continues along the D122 westwards
for 100 metres to a junction with the D185. At
the junction it follows a track, not shown on the
map, between the 2 roads and climbs a hill to
the west 501m high. The GR crosses a col to
the west of the hill, and then descends to the
north west by the old road from Monoblet to
Valestalière, passing above the hamlet of
Pailhès. This road follows the western flank of
the hills overlooking the D185 road, joining it
finally a little before the Col du Rédarès. Follow
the road northwards to the Col.

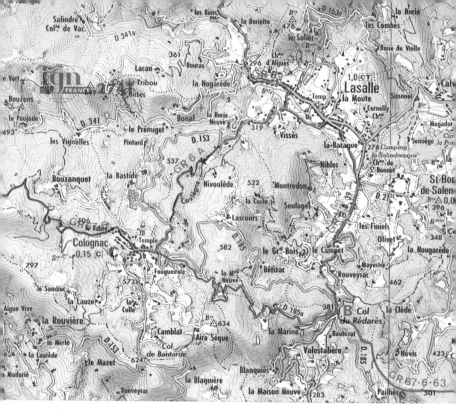

Detour *1hr*

LASALLE

278m.

5Km
1:30

Junction

The GR6A leading northwards to Lasalle joins the GR67 and GR6 at the crossroads.

Detour see left. Follow the waymarking of the GR63 to the north west, taking, beyond the col, the old Lasalle road to the left of the D39. It is possible to rejoin the GR67 at the crossroads east of Colognac by following the GR6A southwards from Lasalle.

From the southern slope of the Col du Rédarès the GR bears westward along the old D185A road. It winds climbing up into a chestnut plantation, passes by La Maison Neuve and joins the D185 again to the east of Colognac. Taking a short cut across a horseshoe bend in the approaches to Colognac, it reaches a crossroads of the D185 with the D153.

Continue along the GR to Colognac.

Signal Towers

In the Cévenol valleys there are many traces of signal towers, some of them isolated, some built on to castles, and placenames like La Fare (meaning a light) or Les Fumades (smoke) show where others have disappeared.

According to Julius Caesar, the Gauls were already using such towers to relay warnings of danger by flaming beacon fires at night or smoke signals by day. It seems likely that these signal towers in the Cévennes date back to the 100 Years War. They are in any case evidence of a collective system of defence against a common enemy who may well have been the English.

These towers are especially numerous in the Vallée Française, and it was clearly possible to signal from the 'Castellas' at Barre-des-Cèvennes to Saint-Étienne-Vallée Française by way of Le Carourgue (finest of the towers still standing), Moissac and La Tour de Lancise, over a distance of some 30 kilometres. And in the valley of the River Salindrenque, Lasalle could exchange signals with the Castellas of Saint-Bonnet, Colognac, Beauvoir and Peyre.

In all, 35 signalling points have been identified, the two extremes of the network being Florac and Anduze, 46 kilometres apart as the crow flies. The House of Anduze, who were very powerful in Languedoc, had thus a very extensive alarm system at their disposal.

R. POUJOL

Near Saint-Germain-de-Calberte

COLOGNAC
⌂ ✕ ♟ ⚓

(see map ref C)
570m
After Colognac, at 600m, the track enters an uninhabited mountainous zone, and gradually climbs up into the upper valley of the Liron stream as far as the Col du Fageas, 1,177m high. The first dwelling to be encountered is on the southern slope of the Col de l'Asclié, 905m high. The hamlet of Bonperrier farther on is occupied only in the summer, but a relais d'étape can be found at La Bessède on the GR6A variant. One must get to Aire-de-Côte at the junction of the GR6 and GR7 to find a gîte d'étape of any consequence.

10Km
3:00

Col du Fageas
1,120m
Possible to go directly to the Col de l'Asclié 20 minutes away by descending the very steep stony slopes of the draille to the north west.

1.5Km
0:20

Col below Le Rocher de l'Aigle
1,096m
Junction The GR61 coming from the east, from Mialet and Anduze, joins the GR67 and GR6.

2Km
0:30

Follow the GR through Colognac. At the first crossroads bear right, to the north west, and beyond the last house at the second crossroads turn left towards Le Fabre. From there take the track descending gently to the west along the southern slope of hill 706, then climb again northwards and cross over a col where the Draille de Margeride goes. Leave the draille, which climbs to the west along the ridge, and continue on the track winding across the northern flank of the mountain, with its extensive views. You will pass by a ruined sheep-fold at Les Fosses, and then the track describes a wide loop to the north east towards a place called Le Camp Barrat. From there the track climbs westward to the northern slope of mountain 1001, and then by a hairpin bend, reaches the crest at the Col de la Baraque, 942m high. Here the GR encounters the Draille de Margeride again and follows it northwards. After skirting a small hill the draille crosses another col at 942m.

Warning Watch the waymarking very carefully. The draille has become increasingly disused and tends to be overgrown with broom. After crossing the col it has been cut through and incorporated in new forestry roads.

The draille continues to climb up along the eastern slope of the Liron mountain to reach the Col du Fageas.

From the col the GR takes a forestry road to the east, passing below Le Fageas, to reach a col at the foot of Le Rocher de l'Aigle.

The GR turns westward, to the left, along the forestry road to the Col de l'Asclié.

Hydrography of the Cévennes

The Cévennes rear up out of the Languedoc plain like one gigantic wall, rising to more than 1,500m in altitude, 50 to 80 kilometres from the sea as the crow flies. The whole of this Cévenol countryside is furrowed by countless ravines, known locally as *'valats'*, in the river basins of the Cèze, the Gardons, the Tarn, Hérault and Dourbie. In areas of schist these ravines carve up the mountains into long narrow ridges or *'Serres'*. In granitic zones the relief is gentler, with rounded summits, where erosion has given rise to enormous blocks of 'erratic' rocks. The rivers of the region empty into the Mediterranean or the Atlantic, with the watershed running through La Croix de Berthel, the Col de Jalcreste, Barre-des-Cévennes, the Col de Marquairès, Mont Aigoual and the Col de l'Homme Mort.

P. MAGNE

Col de l'Asclié
(see map ref D)
905m
There is a spring 100 metres to the south of the col, below the level of the D20 road.

Junction Crossroads of the GR67 and GR6 with the GR61A and the GR6B. To the north, by the D125 road, the GR61A leads to Estréchure and from there joins the GR61 at the Col du Mercou. To the south, the GR6B leads to Notre-Dame-de-la-Rouvière.

2Km
0:45

Detour *2hrs*
NOTRE-DAME-DE-LA-ROUVIÈRE
ⓗ ✕ ⚒
402m

Detour see left. From the Col de l'Asclié follow the waymarking of the GR6B southwards, almost wholly by the road, to Notre-Dame-de-la-Rouvière. It is possible to rejoin the GR67 either at the Col de l'Homme Mort by the GR6C, via Puech Sigal - in 1 hour 45 minutes, or at Bonperrier by the GR6B - in 2 hours 15 minutes.

From the Col de l'Asclié follow the GR to the west on the Draille de Margeride, crossing a bridge over the D20 road. The draille continues to the Col de l'Homme Mort.

Col de l'Homme Mort
(see map ref E)
909m
Junction The GR6C from Notre-Dame-de-la-Rouvière to the south and the GR6A from Les Plantiers to the north join the GR67 and GR6.

Detour *45 mins*
LA BESSÈDE
⌂
650m

Detour see left. From the Col de l'Homme Mort follow the waymarking of the GR6A to the north west, via Le Mas Soubeyran, to La Bessède where it divides into 2 branches. You can return to the GR67 at Bonperrier by the south west branch in 30 minutes.

3.5Km
1:00

Detour *1 hr 45 mins*
LES PLANTIERS

Detour see left. Take the GR6A from the Col de l'Homme Mort to La Bessède, and from

⌂ ⌂ ⚓

404m

there by the northern branch of the GR6A from La Bessède, to Les Plantiers, via Mas Lautal and L'Oultre. The GR6A goes on past the Romanesque Abbey of Saint-Marcel-de-Fontfouillouse and the Col de l'Espinas to rejoin the GR67 and GR6 at about 2 kilometres south east of Aire-de-Côte.

From the Col de l'Homme Mort the GR continues on the Draille de Margeride to the north west and then to the west by way of the north face of the Serre de Lacam.

Junction

A little farther on from the Serre de Lacam the GR6B from Notre-Dame-de-la-Rouvière joins the GR67 and GR6 on the left.

The GR continues to Bonperrier.

Spates in the Cévennes

The Cévenol rainstorms can affect the eastern face of the Massif Central along a 200 to 300 kilometre front, running from the Vivarais to the Cévennes region itself, including the Aigoual range. They can strike at all seasons, even in mid-summer, but are always heaviest from the beginning of September to the end of October, when they reach spectacular and often catastrophic proportions. They Gardons rivers, in particular, typify Cévenol hydrography, dominating as they do a stretch of the adjacent Rhône Valley for not more than 100 to 150 kilometres. Flowing steeply down over an impermeable surface with a high run-off factor, they very rapidly gather virtually the entire rainfall, and consist moreover of a complex network, culminating at a small number of points after roughly equal courses, and hence with simultaneous convergence of the floodwater from each river basin. Spates resulting from short sharp storms in the upper valleys are the most devastating, rising with the speed of lightning, each headed by a wave a metre or metre-and-a-half high. They reach their maximum level within about 3 hours, and recede nearly as fast, the ebb rarely lasting more than an hour.
M. BAUZIL

In the higher reaches drystone sills have been built across the stream beds, as breakwaters, to regulate the flow and enable some of the earth that is washed away to be recovered. The terraced fields are protected from the gathering run-off by conduits which drain the water away, and many of the farmhouses and hamlets have been built up on the mountainsides rather than close to the unpredictable rivers. The Gardons are trout streams, but their banks are also the home of beavers, vegetarian and nocturnal animals who make their burrows there. These animals had disappeared from the rivers on the Atlantic side of the watershed, the Mimente and the Tarnon, but a few individuals taken from the Gardons have been reintroduced there by the National Park.

Bonperrier
(see map ref F)
839km
Hamlet occupied only in summer; sheep-fold; spring at 300m.

Junction The GR6A from Les Plantiers joins the GR67 and GR6 on the right and on the left the GR62 joins the GR67 and GR6 from Valleraugue.

Detour *2 hrs 15 mins*
VALLERAUGUE
🏠 ⌂ 🏕 🍴 🍷 ⚜ 🅱
360m

6Km
2:00

A monument has been raised at the Col du Pas in memory of the Aigoual Maquis.

Detour see left. Follow the GR62 from Bonperrier. It is possible to return to the GR67 and GR6 at the Col du Pas - or Col des Traverses - by the D10 road.

The GR continues to the north west, still following the draille, to the Col du Terme and then the north facing slope of Le Tour. The draille descends by the ridge to the Col du Pas - or Col des Traverses - at the crossroads of the D10 and the D193.

From the north face of the Col du Pas the GR takes a rather badly defined footpath on the left of the road and below the level of the monument. It joins the old Valleraugue road which climbs rather steeply, in hairpin bends, northwards to the ridge at an unnamed col at the junction with the D10d road.

Gold in the Cévennes

Ancient Gaul was famous enough for its gold to earn to the name of *'Gallia Deaurata'*, 'Golden Gaul'. The Gauls knew very well how to extract the gold from the alluvial deposits and sands of the river beds, and the robes of their chiefs were decorated with gold and silver. According to Julius Caesar gold was found in most of the rivers rising in the Massif Central.

In the Gallo-Roman period gold working increased, and the Cévennes region was one of the most productive. The deposits of gold particles carried down by the Rivers Cèze, Gardon and Gagnières are mainly found in the carboniferous basin. It is in the quartz and schist conglomerates at the base of the coal-bearing rock that the precious metal occurs, and when these conglomerates are broken up by the force of the water the quartz and auriferous gravels are carried away by the stream. Gold washing still survives in a few places today.

R. AUBARET

Unnamed Col
(see map ref G)
1,012m

1.5Km
0:30

Junction The GR6A from Les Plantiers via the Col de l'Espinas and Saint-Marcel-de-Fonfouillouse joins the GR67 and GR6 on the left.

AIRE-DE-CÔTE FORESTER'S LODGE
⌂
1,085m
Limited water; the GR

The GR follows the D10d to the north west from the unnamed col as far the col where the Aire-de-Côte forester's lodge is situated.

Beyond the forester's lodge the GR divides, providing 2 routes to the Col Salidès: 1. by the draille - 7 kilometres, or 2. by the forestry road – 9 kilometres

1. The Draille de Margeride, after cutting a

9Km
2:30

approaches the Aigoual massif here, on the Atlantic/Mediterranean watershed; it leaves the Gard department for that of Lozére and enters the Cévennes National Park.

Junction The GR6 separates from the GR67 and makes its way westwards to Mont Aigoual. The GR7 joins the GR67 and follows the same route as far as the approach to the Col de Jalcreste.

Col Salidès
1,014m
The D19 road crosses the GR.

swathe through the forest, follows close to the ridge by fairly steep slopes in the scree. It joins the forestry road again to the west of the Serre du Tarnon.

2. The forestry road, longer by 2 kilometres, winds about to avoid the steeper gradients and intersects the draille where the draille descends to the watering places. It skirts a ravine and goes on below the Serre du Tarnon (see map ref H).

A little beyond the Serre du Tarnon the GR continues along the forestry road which intermingles with the draille. It follows the north eastern face of the mountain to the Col Salidès.

The GR follows the draille from the Col Salidès along the north west side of the ridge to the edge of the Marquairès forest. It skirts the forest to the north east as far as the Col du Marquairès, and crosses the col by going over the tunnel. The GR continues on the draille northwards, gradually climbing up to the

Saint-Germain-de-Calbert

Terrasses

The *'terrasse'* is an almost cylindrical basket, with very slightly bulging sides, woven of chestnut shoots with a rim of bitter-almond, which is widely used in the Cévennes.

It has a long history, this basket, and is actually a 'dosser' or back-pannier; the local people call it the *'panier de la terre'* the *'terraïrou'* or 'earth basket'. They still use it today, for carrying manure up to their gardens, for example, or bringing in the vegetables, but originally it served as a measure (like a bushel basket in Britain), and this is why they still call it an earth basket.

In the old days a labourer doing a day's work for the squire or the priest or some other important personage would be paid in food - chestnuts perhaps - or in earth. And the basket was the measure: he filled it with earth from his employer's land, from some corner that was not easily cultivated, and carried it home to his own small plot, where he emptied out the earth on to some stony slope. And there, held in by a low dry-stone wall, the earth he brought, basketful by basketful, day after day, gradually became a small artificial meadow or vineyard or hanging garden - one of those marvellous terraced fields know as *'traversiers'* in this area, as *'barres'* around Chambord, *'accols'* over towards Ardèche, *'bancels'* elsewhere, and *'faïsses'* almost everywhere in the Cévennes.

JEAN-PIERRE CHABROL,
Le Crève-Cévenne

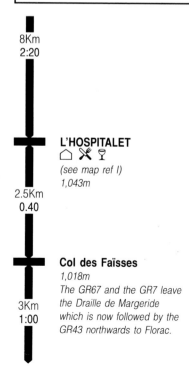

8Km
2:20

western edge of the small causse of L'Hospitalet, following it closely and giving views over the Tarnon Valley and the Causse Méjean. Now clearly waymarked, now a cart track, the draille is easy to follow here. Going northwards at first, it bears to the north east to join the D9 road at the approach to L'Hospitalet below some ruiniform rocks.

L'HOSPITALET
⌂ ✗ ♀
(see map ref I)
1,043m

2.5Km
0.40

From L'Hospitalet take the GR northwards, first of all following the draille which runs along the eastern side of the D9 road. At the place where the road closes on to the eastern edge of the causse, steeply overlooking the Vallée Française, follow the road. The GR passes the Col de Solpérière and continues on to the Col des Faïsses.

Col des Faïsses
1,018m
The GR67 and the GR7 leave the Draille de Margeride which is now followed by the GR43 northwards to Florac.

3Km
1:00

The GR leaves the D9 road at the Col des Faïsses and follows a track on the right to the south east. After crossing the plateau it descends on the right in a hairpin bend, and winds round the Can Noire to reach the D983 road at the north western approach to Barre-des-Cévennes - reached by following the road to the right.

The Corniche des Cévennes

At L'Hospitalet the GR encounters an important tourist highway, the 'Corniche des Cévennes', which links Saint-Jean-du-Gard with Florac, via Le Pompidou and the Col des Faïsses.

In a memorandum of 25 January 1725, about selection of a communication route between the provinces of Languedoc and Auvergne, there is already mention of this axis linking Montpellier and Clermont by way of the Gévaudan and passing through Anduze, Saint-Jean-de-Gardonnenque, Florac, Mende and Saint-Chély. The memorandum expands for several pages on the difficulty of the journey for heavy wagons and stage coaches, but insists on the commercial importance of this route for the transport of worsted, serge and other textiles manufactured in the Gévaudan, for which, it says, 'there is so much demand throughout the whole of France'. It therefore proposes that the Crown should improve and extend this line of communication.

In the 19th century this royal route became the national highway N107 from Nîmes to Saint-Flour, before being downgraded in favour of the route through the Vallée Borgne and Le Marquairès a little to the south.

The title 'Corniche des Cévennes' first appeared in 1925 in a bulletin of the Cévenol Club. Since 1927 the Saint-Jean-du-Gard section of the Club has taken pains to rehabilitate this tourist route, which some people were at one time suggesting should be called the 'Amethyst Corniche'.

E. BRINGER

Barre-des-Cévennes

Barre must certainly owe its origin to military needs. In the high Middle Ages an ancient castle stood on the 'Castellas' that dominates the area, with a tall tower for exchanging signals with several other strongholds (see note above on 'Signal Towers').

In the 13th century a *'Château-Neuf'* or 'new castle' was built below the Castellas, which still exists in its 16th century form. Constructed in the centre of a fortified section of the town, the 'Barrium', this castle was the seat of a prominent seigniory.

Barre has always been an important agricultural and commercial market town. The country people came here to sell or barter their homespun cloth, the famous 'caddis' or worsted, woven on the farms from wool spun by hand. In 1736 there were still 65 weavers producing worsted in the Vallée Française.

That Barre was built to a regular town-plan - 100 houses, 50 on each side of the street - is incontestable: houses of several storeys, standing cheek by jowl, with arcades running the length of the covered walkways. And this in spite of the town's mixed economy, both mercantile and agricultural. Each craftsman or shopkeeper had two doors to his house, one opening on to the street, the other out to the countryside; and alleyways, some of them running through a sort of tunnel under the houses, gave access to the gardens.

Most of the present houses in Barre date from the 15th, 16th and 17th centuries, and constitute one of the most beautiful examples of urban architecture in the Cévennes.

R. POUJOL.

BARRE-DES-CÉVENNES
🏠 ⌂ 🛆 ✕ ☎ 🛈

(see map ref J)
915m

The GR72 bears off to the left, to the north east, at the second fork towards Le Pont du Tarn and Villefort.

This road, the old road from Barre-des-Cévennes to Saint-Germain-de-Calberte, goes over the ridge which separates the Vallée Française to the south from the Vallée de la Mimente to the north, following the Atlantic/Mediterranean watershed. Keeping to a height between 900 and

8Km
2:20

Follow the GR to the south east and at the first fork do not take the D983 descending on the right to the Vallée Française, but climb to the left as far as the second fork, with its wayside calvary.

At this second fork the GR follows the D13 road to the south east, ignoring the D62 on the left.

The GR continues on the D13 to the crossroads at Plan de Fontmort.

1,000m, it overlooks the whole region and provides extensive views over the Cévennes, of Mont Lozère to the north, and the Aigoual to the south. A footpath parallel to the road allows one partly to avoid walking on the tarmac.

Plan de Fontmort
896m
Monument commemorating one of the battles of the War of the Camisards; there is also a standing stone.
From the Plan de Fontmort 2 roads go to the south east, one on each side of the Gardon of Saint-Martin-de-Lansuscle Valley. The D162 goes to the north to Cassagnas 5 kilometres away on the N106, where there are buses to Alès and Florac.

3Km
1:00

The GR continues on the old Barre-des-Cévennes to Saint-Germain-de-Calberte road northwards for 100 metres. There it takes a shortcut across a hairpin bend and then continues along the road.

Down from the road at a place called Claroudens there is a quartz menhir and a neolithic coffin burial.

This beautiful road continues to a junction of paths.

Junction of paths
(see map ref K)
1,013m
The GR67A leaves the GR67 and GR7 to the west of Mont Mars.

7Km
2:00

Alternative route. The GR67A follows the old road to Saint-Germain-de-Calberte. It continues in a gentle descent to the southern slope of Mont Mars as far as the Col de la Pierre Plantée, with its standing stone, at 891m. Near a reservoir, 2 kilometres beyond the col, take a track on the right to the cluster of buildings at Le Serre de la Can, from where a path goes down through the woods to Saint-Germain-de-Calberte.

SAINT-GERMAIN-DE-CALBERTE
⌂ ⚏ 🛈
I480m

5.5Km
1:45

The GR leaves Saint-Germain-de-Calberte by the D984 road to the south for about 500 metres, then turns to the right on to a track connecting Les Faysses and Les Moles. This track, running almost parallel to the D984, cuts across the D13, goes on above La Liquière, and then a little beyond La Liquiérolle, rejoins

The Legend of the Dead Woman

In very ancient times a fairy had made her home on Mont Mars. Now this fairy had a very bad temper, so violent that they called her a 'hell-cat'. The story goes that a widow woman from near Saint-Germain-de-Calberte had, despite her advanced age, committed a sin and given birth to a baby. As a punishment the fairy condemned her to tear an enormous rock from the slopes of Mont des Laupies and to wander for ever until she died, with her donkey, this load, and her baby. The old woman set off with her heavy burden, but the baby was still too young to endure the stresses of such a journey, and soon it died, at the col named Plan de Fontmort - *'d'enfant mort'* (dead baby).

Continuing on her endless travels the poor woman came to the valley of a stream that runs into the River Gardon-de-Saint-Germain. Just to the south of the village she tried to cross the river, but the donkey lost its footing and was drowned, which is how the place came to be called Négase - *'noie âne'* (drowned ass). Still struggling painfully on her way and crushed by the weight of the stone, the old woman started to climb up the mountain. But before she got to the top, exhausted, she dropped her burden and fell down and died on the ridge that is now called after her: 'Montagne de la Vieille Morte' (the Old Woman who died), where there is also a standing stone known as the 'Pierre de la Vieille'.

---

the road. Cross it, and descend as far as yet another road running alongside the Gardon de Saint-Germain. Follow it on the left, north eastwards, then cross the gardon by a footbridge and continue to the Pont de Burgen.

PONT DE BURGEN

⌂

(see map ref a)
274m

4Km
1:20

Follow the GR67A eastwards along a road down to the bottom of a valley, then climb again in hairpin bends to La Fregeyre. From there the GR makes its way to Les Longagnes, goes round a small hill to the north at altitude mark 664 to a col and the standing stone known as the 'Pierre de la Vieille'.

Pierre de la Vieille
656m
Junction The GR67A is joined by the GR67B from Canteloup via the hamlets of Les Abrits and Serre.

2Km
0:40

The GR67A and GR67B follow the motor road to the east south east for 2 kilometres as far as a reservoir.

Reservoir
(see map ref O)
750m
The GR67A and GR67B join the GR67 coming from Les Ayres.

Junction of Paths
(see map ref K)
1,013m
Situated west of Mont Mars.

4Km
1:20

Col des Laupies
1,000m
In the middle of a clearing a monument commemorating the rehabilitation of the old royal road.

4Km
1:15

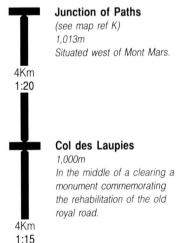

The GR67 leaves the old Saint-Germain-de-Calberte road to follow a farm track on the left which skirts the northern slopes of Mont Mars. Close to altitude mark 1,112, some 3 kilometres from the footpath junction, leave the farm track for a path on the right - not shown on the map - which descends through the Fontmort forest to rejoin the old royal road of Saint-Germain-de-Calberte to Florac at the Col des Laupies.

Follow the old royal road to the north east, crossing over the northern slope of the mountain to the Col de la Vergnasse. The GR then continues along a forestry road which describes a wide curve to the foot of a large col.

Warning When there is fog, keep to the forestry road which turns to the west and continue for 2 kilometres past the Solpéran forester's lodge to the Col de Jalcreste.

At the foot of the large col the GR turns right and continues eastwards up to the col.

The Legend of the Buried Bell

The most important massif between Mont Lozère, 1,762m high, and Mont Aigoual, 1,560m, is known as Mont Mars. We may guess there was once a shrine here to the god Mercury, or Mercoire as the ancient Gauls called him, and the name got shortened to 'Merc', and later to 'Mars'. Mont Mars is really a long plateau, with two summits, the beacons of Cabanis, 1,250m high, at one end and Saint-Clément, 1,150m, at the other. The name Saint-Clément suggests that in about the 8th century missionary monks may have replaced a Gaulish shrine there by a Christian chapel, around which a little village grew up.

But how and why did that village suddenly lose all its inhabitants? If we can believe the legend, the Gévaudan area lived in terror of the roving bands of English soldiers who were then ravaging France. Learning that Du Guesclin, who had undertaken to drive the English out, had just been killed at Châteauneuf-de-Randon in Lozère, the panic-striken people of Saint-Clément decided to leave their village rather than face the threat of pillage, and fled to the Causses with their flocks. Before they left, the village priest had the church bell taken down, and everyone placed whatever valuables they had inside it. The bell was then buried, very deep, and covered over with *lauzes* and stones. No one knows if the people of Saint-Clément reached their destination, only that none of them ever returned to the village.

Over the centuries the story of the bell has tempted a lot of hopefuls to climb up the Mont Mars armed with picks and shovels, but so far the rough ground has not yielded up its secret.

Large col
(see map ref L)
918m
The GR7 separates from the GR67 and continues northwards to the Col de Jalcreste then on to Le Bleymard and La Bastide-Puylaurent.

6Km
2:00

Detour *20 mins*
COL DE JALCRESTE
🏠 △ ✕ 🚉 🚌
Follow the GR7 along the draille northwards to the col.

LES AYRES
△ ⵏ
(see map ref M)
780m

1:40

The GR67 turns to the right again from the large col and follows the draille du Gévaudan to the south.

Warning The draille follows a succession of ridges which, until Les Ayres, are uninhabited.

The GR climbs steeply up to the top of the Cayla, 1,068m high, and leaves the draille here, turning right to go down to the Col des Abeilles. From the col take a track on the left following the southern slope of the mountain eastwards, overlooking Saint-André-de-Lancize. The GR joins the draille again and crosses the D984 to the Col de la Croix de Bourel at 783m. It continues southwards, almost parallel to the D54, to the hamlet, Les Ayres.

Warning Beyond Les Ayres it is difficult in bad weather to retain a sense of direction on the draille, and the slabs of the schist are slippery. It is much safer to continue to the Col du Pradel by the GR67B alternative route.

Alternative route The GR67B follows the D54 road from Les Ayres southwards to Le Pendédis.

LE PENDÉDIS
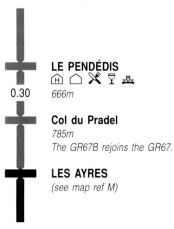
666m

From Le Pendédis the GR follows the D13 westward to the Col du Pradel.

0.30

Col du Pradel
785m
The GR67B rejoins the GR67.

LES AYRES
(see map ref M)

The GR67 follows the D54 for a few metres, then as it leaves the hamlet joins the draille again, going at first through woods and then through thickets of bushes.

The 'Logue' at Les Ayres

A very special type of fair used to be held at Les Ayres, on the road from Pendédis to Jalcreste, a kilometre before you reach the Col de la Croix de Bourel or du Bourreau (donkey) above Saint-André-de-Lancise. This fair, or 'Logue' as it was called locally, was where day labourers came to be hired for seasonal jobs like collecting silkworms or chestnut gathering, harvesting corn or picking grapes. First there was the 'Big Fair', then a week later the 'Little Fair' for the people who had not been able to make a deal at the first one. Those who had been hired wore some visible sign of their contract: a piece of ribbon or an ear of corn, say, to signify silkworms or grain harvesting, and also to show they were no longer for hire.

4Km
1:15

On IGN maps the draille in this area is labelled 'Draille du Languedoc'.
On this stretch the draille is less and less used for the seasonal movement of stock and in places is little more than a network of tracks among the bushes. Following the ridge line of the mountain closely is the best guide. In

The GR joins the D13 road to the Col du Pradel.

Sheep Bells on the Draille

Each type of bell has its own 'song'. The ones called sonals say 'montadoun', 'montadoun', 'up to the mountains, the mountains'; the clapas say 'davalarem, davalarem', 'down to the valley, the valley'; and the piques reply 'retornarem, retornarem', 'we shall return again, again and again'.

The bells are also meant to be decorative, and the shepherds are very proud of them as well as their music. They are hung from wide collars that are much more highly decorated than those used for the bells worn in the pastures. In the old days they were modelled or carved with a great variety of motifs: geometric patterns, flowers, rosettes. Today the shepherds simply paint them in different colours, especially reds and blues.

Finally, the transhumance bells had the same sort of magical power as church bells. They were supposed to protect the flock against all sorts of dangers: against sorcerers and their evil spells, and against storms. Today this sense of magic has practically disappeared, and the bells are merely considered as ornamental, and as a means of keeping the flock together.

To the sheep the transhumance bell signals that it is time to set off for the mountains; the shepherds call it 'the song of departure'. Once the flock have these bells on they become more difficult to control except when actually heading for the mountain pastures.

ANNE-MARIE BRISEBARRE
Shepherds of the Cévennes

good conditions this route is very pleasant with splendid views.

Col du Pradel
785m

Junction The GR67B from Pendédis rejoins the GR67.

1.5Km
0:30

The GR leaves the col by the track to Cabanemagre, and then by the draille turning right and going southwards along the ridge. It then turns to the east at altitude mark 842, and follows a road for 600 metres south eastwards as far as a sort of col close by a placed called Canteloup.

Canteloup
(see map ref N)
755m

Warning In bad weather avoid the Montagne de la Vieille Morte on the GR67 and use the GR67B alternative route southwards, rejoining the GR67 close to a reservoir.

1:50

Alternative route to the reservoir. The GR67B, close to Canteloup, goes directly southwards and becomes a road suitable for vehicles. The road runs along the western edge of the mountain, overlooking the Gardon de Saint-Germain valley, and passes close by the hamlets of Les Travers, Serre, and Les Abrits to Pierre de la Vieille.

Pierre de la Vieille
656m

Junction The GR67B joins the GR67A alternative route from Saint-Germain-de-Calberte and Pont de Burgen (see map ref A)

0:30

From Pierre de la Vieille the GR67B (and GR67A) continue east south east for 2 kilometres on the motor road to a reservoir.

3.5Km
1:00

At Canteloup the GR67 leaves the road to follow the draille to the south west flank of a rounded hill. The draille reaches a large col, climbs a hill beyond it at altitude mark 866, and from the next col climbs through some bushes on to the crest of the Vieille Morte. Just below the summit the GR crosses a small col.

Small col
900m
The GR44B joins the GR67 from Saint-Martin-de-Boubaux and Bessèges to the east.

1.5Km
0:20

From the col the GR climbs to the summit of the Vieille Morte, 920m, where you will find the ruins of a chapel. The GR descends southwards and crosses through a wood to the Saint-Martin-de-Boubaux forestry road.

Junction with another branch of the GR44B linking with the branch at the small col.

The GR follows the forestry road southwards to a reservoir.

Reservoir
(see map ref 0)
750m

Junction The GR67 joins the GR67A alternative route from Saint-Germain-de-Calberte and the GR67B bad weather alternative route from Canteloup (see map ref N) and Pierre de la Vieille.

4Km
1:15

The GR follows the motor road again as far as an isolated farm, at 636m, called Le Pereyret. It continues, still on the road, along the ridge where the draille goes, overlooking the drainage basin of the tributaries of the Salandre and providing glimpses of the Gardon de Mialet valley. Take care at the junction north of La Clède du Pas to go to the right. After a hairpin bend the GR crosses a large col close to a place called Campmau.

CAMPMAU
⌂
528km

The GR follows a forestry road southwards to the Col d'Uglas and leaves the Lozère department to re-enter Gard. Before reaching the col, the GR leaves the road for a footpath on the right descending southwards through thickets of bushes towards the D160 road. The path reaches the road at a bridge over the Rules stream at altitude mark 373, and cuts across the road to the hamlet of Les Aigladines.

3Km
0:45

Les Aigladines
(see map ref P)
390m
The route leaves the region of the Hautes Cévennes for the valley of the Gardon de Mialet.

3Km
1:00

Follow the GR along the draille, now become a road, from Les Aigladines and descend, first to the south and then to the south east along the western flank of Mont Camp. At Clapiers, 2.5 kilometres farther on, the GR emerges on to the D50 road, which goes on to the left as far as Le Pont des Camisards at the same altitude as the first houses in Mialet.

Les Aigladines
'Profiting from the ties already formed between the Cévennes and the textile towns of the plain, Nîmes and Montpellier, and making use of the many craftsmen of the region - the carders, weavers, or the shoemakers - the Reformation penetrated the mountain region by the customary routes, the valleys of the Gardons. Little by little, from 1540 until 1570, it took hold in the steeply terraced valleys, but made no headway on the great limestone plateaux to the west. It was in this hamlet of Les Aigladines that the first synod of the Reformed Churches of eastern Languedoc was held, in 1560'.
PH. JOUTARD

MIALET
🏠 Å ✕ ⚒

(see map ref Q)
161m
*At Le Pont des Camisards
the GR61 from Saint-Jean-du-
Gard and the junction with
the GR67 near Le Rocher de
l'Aigle rejoins the GR67. The
GR67 and the GR61 follow
the same route to Anduze.*

2.5Km
0:45

As it leaves Mialet the GR turns to the right on to a track between the D50 road and the Gardon, rejoining the road at Trabuc. Follow the road for several metres southwards, then take the old track on the left to the south east. It climbs upwards and then descends gradually towards the hamlet of Mas Soubeyran.

Mas Soubeyran
180m
*The Musée du Désert (or
Museum of the Wilderness),
founded in 1910 by the
Société de l'Histoire du
Protestantisme Française,
occupies a group of old
houses in the hamlet of Mas
Soubeyran, one of which was
the birthplace of the
Camisard leader Roland.
Contains a very large
number of the Camisards'
war souvenirs, and offers
moving evidence of their
resistance to the severe
religious oppression which
was so heavily inflicted upon
this region. Every year on the
first Sunday in September
several thousand Protestants,
many from far away, gather
here in remembrance.*

*It is no longer possible to
walk along the railway line as
it is now frequently used as
a scenic railway.*

6.5Km
2:00

The GR descends to join the D50 road and leaves it almost immediately for the old track running below Luziers along the bank of the Gardon. The GR then rejoins the road and yet again leaves it almost immediately, on the left, meeting up with it once more after Pradinas and following it then for about 1 kilometre. After a hairpin bend, 200 metres beyond the top of the slope, on the right, follow the draille, now tarred, towards the north east. Join the D129 at Montsauve and continue on it southwards to Anduze.

ANDUZE
🏠 ⌂ Å ✕ ⟁ ⚒ ▭
🛈

135m
*The GR67 ends here. It is
possible to continue to the
south east towards Beaucaire
on the GR6.*

THE TOUR DU MONT AIGOUAL

WALK 3

GR66 Introduction

The Cévennes National Park was established in 1970 to conserve the balance of nature and maintain the rural economy of the Cévenol uplands; also to enable all those so inclined to get to know this countryside and make friends with its inhabitants, who keep the region alive.

To explore the Cévennes on foot is certainly the best way of making acquaintance with such unspoilt country. This is especially true of the Aigoual and the Lingas, great granite 'shields' where the woodland has been restored by the famous pioneer of ecology and forestry expert Georges Fabre, and where the extensive network of paths and sheep tracks, like the magnificent old houses, testify to centuries of human enterprise and toil.

The Tour du Mont Aigoual footpath was created and waymarked by the Comité National des Sentiers de Grande Randonnée, and the National Park has supported the project and shared in the establishment of *Gîtes d'Étape* at Aire-de-Côte, Dourbies and L'Espérou.

The popularity of this new way of exploring the countryside, among young people as well as their elders, shows very clearly how well it fulfils the aspiration so many people feel today: of living in harmony with the environment instead of exploiting it. Walkers are made welcome here, whether they come from close at hand or - since the long distance European Footpath 4 also crosses Mont Aigoual - from afar. So look out for all the fascinating sites and signs that testify to the past history of the region; and respect the work of its farmers and shepherds, who will be ready to greet and help you as best they can. The natural landscape here may lack the majesty of the higher mountain summits, but is equally worthy of your interest and appreciation. Here you will be entering a land ruled only by silence and the wind, so enjoy your journey!

Geological Sketch

All along the eastern face of the Massif Central the ancient rock systems, with their very extensive Secondary covering, went through a phase of dislocation attributable, as Fabre suggested in 1873, to pressures from the Pyrenean upheavals of the Tertiary period. This Tertiary folding split up the whole region into a series of monoclinal blocks with the faults running in an east/west direction. In most of the troughs remains of the Secondary system, which once stretched over the whole region, still subsist, as evidenced by the fragments occurring here and there on the down side of certain blocks.

In the southern Cévennes the upthrow side of the blocks faces south and the dip northward. This southern group includes the Aigoual with the River Hérault and Bonheur stream on its southern border, the Suquet bordered by the River Dourbie, and finally the Lingas-Saint-Guiral chain overlooking the river valleys of the Arre and the Virenque. In the lower areas stretching northward there is extensive evidence of the Secondary cover in the form of small *causses* in the vicinity of Barre. The upheaved blocks, and especially the higher ones which form a large part of the Aigoual and Lingas, are of granite, the under side of each merging, more or less, with the post-Hercynian surface.

On the north the Aigoual massif is bordered by the Cabrillac fault, where a little band of sandstone is squeezed in. South of the break the granite surface rises to a height of 1,500m, which is maintained as far as the Aigoual Observatory at 1,567m.

On the south, the Aigoual block is cut through by the great east/west fault of the Serreyrède. This fracture has been deepened by the upper reaches of the River Hérault, which has carved out a straight and narrow V-shaped valley. The deepening has taken place so fast that the tributary valleys, one of which is regarded as the source of the Hérault, have been left suspended, forming a series of waterfalls. This fault is marked out by a line of silver-bearing lead mines, now abandoned, extending westwards towards Lanuéjols along the edge of the Causse Noir. Its escarpment forms the end of the little Croix-de-Fer-La Fajole chain, with the small sand and limestone *causses* of Camprieu and Saint-Sauveur-des-Pourcils at its foot. From this low level the slope runs steadily up again towards the south, with evidence of sandstone recurring almost as far as the Suquet signal tower, showing that the whole of this face belongs to the post-Hercynian structure. From the roughly even level of the ridge - ranging from 1,302m to 1,393m - a very steep slope plunges down to the River Dourbie. To the west and south west the post-Hercynian surface runs down under the Causse Bégon and the Causse du Larzac.

The Lingas crest is not so much a sharp ridge as a humped plateau, with its successive heights of the Montagne d'Aulas at 1,422m, La Lusette at 1,445m, Peyrebesse at 1,410m and the rounded dome of Saint-Guiral at 1,366m overlooking the valley of the River Arre.

The monoclinal and faulted structure of the Aigoual, Suquet and Lingas shows the preponderant role of the post-Hercynian surface on the down side of these blocks.

FROM H. BAULIG
Le Plateau Central de la France

Wildlife in the Forests

In this region the health and growth of the forests depends not only on natural causes, but also on human intervention. Whether we cut down trees or plant new ones, build roads or start fires, we have a determining influence. And many other factors are involved: the kind of soil, the climatic conditions, the competition between different species, with some depending on the shelter of the trees for development while others suffocate there and disappear. The forest does not just consist of trees standing side by side: dead leaves and branches pile up and rot down, there are plants and herbs, creepers and bushes, toadstools, insects, springs, animals that feed, make paths, leave their traces. There are plenty of small mammals: shrews, voles, dormice, squirrels. Badgers feed on roots, wild berries, acorns, beech nuts and even on little animals, marking out their territory with their droppings, and from time to enlarging their sett which ends up revealing its presence by a great heap of banked up earth. In June when they are raising their cubs, foxes can most often be seen. Martens, too, live in the forests, while the stoats (or ermine) prefer the open grassland of the summits. Genets, being strictly nocturnal are harder to see - considered a rare species in France as a whole, they are fairly numerous here, but strictly protected.

Until red deer were reintroduced on the Atlantic-facing slopes of Mont Aigoual - in 1960, 10 years before the creation of the National Park - wild boar were the only large mammals here, feeding on grass, tubers, berries, chestnuts and smaller animals. They had virtually disappeared during most of the 19th century, but since the reafforestation have become plentiful again.

Red deer were also introduced by the Park into the northern half of the massif, and also to the west of the Lingas, where roe deer have joined them. And for both species the forest provides both shelter and the hiding places they need.

Mouflon were acclimatised around 1954-55 on the southern face of Mont Aigoual, but after making a good start their numbers have been considerably reduced by shooting and poaching. However the combined efforts of the National Park and responsible huntsmen over the past few years have brought the number up again to over 100 animals.

The monotony of plantations consisting of one type of tree only (that is, a single species) is not conducive to bird life - they much prefer a mixture of broadleaf and conifer. The common buzzard and the goshawk both establish territories in these forests, where the mistle thrush, wood pigeon and robin are at home. Migrants like the short-toed eagle and honey buzzard also nest in the forests but go off to hunt their prey in more open country. Crossbills particularly favour the fir forests, and coal tits, crested tits, wrens and black woodpeckers too are well adapted to life among the conifers.

The drailles still provide an open passage for sheep through the new plantations, running from col to col along the ridges. Mont Aigoual is crossed by two of these ancient transhumance routes, the Draille d'Aubrac and the Draille de la Margeride. On the Aigoual massif itself a few sheep still come up each year from the lower Cévennes, from around Ganges, Le Vigan, Lasalle, Saint-Jean-du-Gard, Surmène, Saint-André-de-Valborgne, Saint-Hippolyte-du-Fort. They mostly spend the summers on the Lingas, in the valley of the Dourbie, and on the northern face of Mont Aigoual around Cabrillac, Massevaques and Les Fons. To other reasons for the decline in transhumance - such as changes in the overall economy of Languedoc, declining population in the lower valleys, reduction of livestock numbers and the shortage of shepherds - one must add here the reafforestation of the massif, which has greatly reduced the amount of grazing land available.

Near L'Aubaret

WALK 3

L'ESPÉROU

⌂ ⛺ 🍴 🍷 🚠 🚌

1,222m

The estimated walking time for the 25km to Dourbies is 7hrs 15 mins.

The GRs 7, 60 and 71 follow the same route as the GR66 as far as La Baraque-de-Tabusse with the GR71 continuing as far as Le Saint-Guiral.

7Km

The GRs 7 and 60 leave the GRs 66 and 71 on the left, to the south east.

The description of the route takes the village of L'Espérou as its starting point, being the centre of communications at the centre of the Aigoual massif and situated at the crossroads of the N586 road from Valleraugue to Meyrueis and the D48 and D548 to Le Vigan, the D151 to Dourbies and the D55 and D269 to the Col de la Serreyède and L'Aigoual.

Leave the crossroads in the centre of L'Espérou south eastwards by the Draille d'Aubrac. After 400 metres take a track on the right to a small valley, follow it down to the Pueylong stream and proceed along the right bank to the crossing. The GR66 continues along a path which climbs a gully southwards to La Baraque-de-Tabusse, a small ruined shelter at a forestry track crossing.

The GR follows the forestry track on the right to the junction with the D48 road at the Pont des Vaquiers over the Dourbie. It crosses the bridge and goes along the D48 for about 50 metres in the direction of the Col du Minier but leaves the road for a newly opened path on the right, which follows a line concentric to that of the D48, to a road suitable for motor

---

Climate of the Aigoual

The mantle of winter snow covering Mont Aigoual is not often deep or lasting. Extremely violent west winds, often reaching 65 miles an hour, sweep the snow from the summits, piling it up in ravines to the east and south. Nevertheless it can be as much as a metre thick when brought by the wind off the sea. In all, the snowfall here is reckoned to average 60 days a year. Frost, on the other hand, averages 130 to 150 days between October and the end of April. Hoarfrost is frequent above 1,300m and can be very thick, as much as 0.92 having been observed by a Forestry Commission inspector.

The Aigoual massif stands on the watershed, with the River Hérault hurtling down to the Mediterranean on one side and the Tarnon and the Jonte with its tributaries Brèze and Béthuzon answering the pull of the Atlantic on the other. Its annual rainfall is the highest in the Cévennes, as much as 2.27 metres spread over an average 166 days, though varying enormously from season to season and year to year.

AFTER P. MARRES

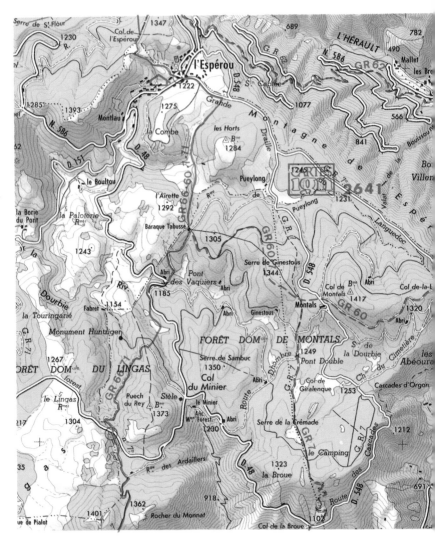

vehicles. The GR follows the road across a tributary of the Dourbie and a little farther on climbs a newly marked out path on the left to the Huntziger monument track, and from there, the Fabret track. This good track bears south and after about 1,500 metres cuts the main forestry road no. 7B.

Forestry road no. 7B

After having crossed the important forestry road no. 7B, the Fabret track, about 500

metres farther on to the south, joins the forestry road no. 7 from the Lingas. The GR follows it for some distance to the south west, keeping to an altitude between 1,200m and 1,300m and overlooking the western slope of the deep Salagosse Valley. After 2 hairpin bends in the beech forest it reaches the Col des Portes, with views largely to the south. At the point where the track bears to the north, at the foot of the Croupe de Ribaldès, 1,432m, the GR

8Km

leaves it on the left for a poor track climbing up southwards to the Fontfroide track which it follows to the left. A little farther on, on the right, the GR joins the new Montlouvier upper track (not shown on the map), and soon afterwards joins the old mule track on the left which descends and passes a little above the half ruined Montlouvier house. The mule track climbs up again and leads into a forestry track. The forestry track climbs eastwards to the left

The Bonheur Valley

This valley sits in a broad corridor between the massif of La Caumette and La Fajole to the north, and the Suquet to the south. Up stream it takes the shape of a shallow basin through which the Bonheur stream dawdles along beside the ruined monastery of Bonahuc, known locally as Bonheur and now engulfed in peaty marshes that at Whitsuntide gleam with a dazzling range of orchids, and later with the downy white tufts of cotton grass, where sphagnum mosses lurk and sundews sparkle with sticky droplets to tempt unwary flies.

Near Camprieu, where the Bonheur reaches the bed of Liassic limestone in the valley bottom, its waters dive into a natural tunnel, reappear briefly in the hollow of the Aven de Balset where the stream makes a right-angled bend, before finally plunging down through fissures in the limestone. After a winding underground course through some 4 kilometres of caverns the river emerges at the Bramabiau falls, 700 metres from where it disappeared, on the side of a ravine stretching back up the slope which has cut through the limestone to a depth of 100 metres.

At the northern end of the valley the River Trévezel, draining the spongy depths of a peat bog, winds through a splendid landscape where the battalions of fir and spruce in the Lagre forest are reminiscent of the Rockies. Parts of the little causse between the Trévezel and Bramabiau have been cleared for agriculture, but only around Camprieu.

Between the valleys of the Trévezel and the Dourbie the *ubacs,* or north facing slopes are clothed with beech. Nearer the tops a few hayfields line the hollows and basins of the streams running into the Trévezel, but the south facing *adret* above the Dourbie is treeless moorland, bare of all but heather and broom.

BASED ON P. MARRES AND R. VACQUIER

and soon, after a hairpin bend, rejoins the upper Montlouvier track which skirts the southern slope of La Lusette, 1,445m high. After about 2 kilometres the GR reaches the Col de l'Homme Mort.

Col de l'Homme Mort
1,300m
Monument commemorating opening of forestry road to Alzon; crossed by forestry road no. 7.

Some metres to the north of the monument the GR follows a path in the forestry plantations to the north west and after 200 metres joins the forestry track again. The track, for about 3 kilometres, follows the northern slope of the mountain, 1,410m high and nicknamed 'Les Trois Quilles', in a generally south western direction. The forestry track leads to a crossroads east of Le Saint-Guiral at altitude mark 1,366m.

10Km

At the crossroads the GR66 separates from the GR71 which skirts the peak of Le Saint-Guiral, descends

At the col several metres farther west a footpath descends westwards through broom bushes down to a stream. It descends directly to the north, following the left bank of the gully,

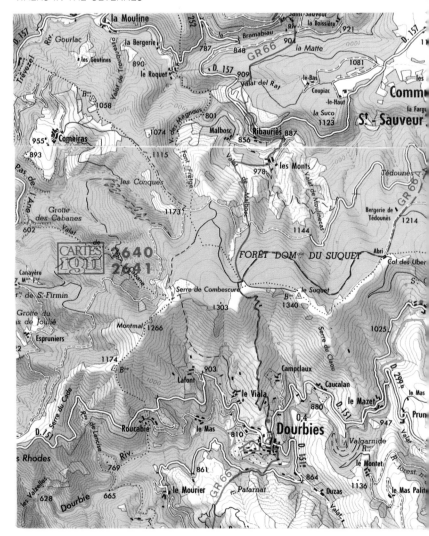

*northwards for about 2
kilometres along a forestry
track as far as a hairpin
bend where it bears
obliquely to the west and
leaves the forest.*

to a small col standing out to the north of the
isolated Ressançon farm. From there a motor
road descends in hairpin bends and crosses
the Crouzoulous stream to the hamlet called La
Rouvière. Going into the hamlet, in front of the
wayside cross, climb the old Dourbies road.
Beyond the col with the wayside cross the old
road descends to the river Dourbie in a north
easterly direction, and after crossing an old
bridge, joins the D151A in front of a cottage.

The Dourbie Valley

This valley starts as a wide basin, its floor of sandy sediments bare in places and broken up by erosion, between the forests of Montals and Faubel on the east and north respectively, and the saddles of the eastern Lingas, previously felled. Here you sink into a peaty soil that a few new conifer plantations are endeavouring to reclaim. The valley then opens up on a soil of granite, also much decomposed, enabling a few fields of rye and potatoes to flourish around the hamlets. Below La Borie-du-Pont the river begins to meander through winding gorges. Around Dourbies, at 897m altitude, chestnut woods fill the valleys of tributary streams and cover the mountain spurs that run steeply down to the winding river, which cuts through an impressive defile to the west of the village, between cliffs of quartz-bearing schist. Its course then tends suddenly downward, dropping 160 metres in 3.5 kilometres. A dam built in 1952 on the Rocher de Bassel, less than 4 kilometres from Saint-Jean-du-Bruel, provides a source of drinking water for this whole area.

Going up the Dourbie valley towards the Lingas and the Saint-Guiral peak, the lower slopes have been terraced, with rows of oak trees sheltering farms, now mostly being abandoned. Higher up, a magnificent forest of beech, spruce, and fir covers the slopes, and west of the Col de l'Homme Mort the forest closes in and overruns some of the higher farms which once were little islands of cultivation, with the usual small plots of rye, potatoes and hay.

FROM P. MARRES AND R. VACQUIER

DOURBIES

867m

The estimated walking time for the 11 kilometres to La Pierre Plantée is 3hrs 15 mins.

Junction

The GR66A alternative route via Camprieu leaves the GR66 obliquely to the north east.

Col du Suquet

1,280m

50 metres farther east the GR follows the footpath downstream to a footbridge over the river, and then climbs up as far as Dourbies.

At the crossroads to the north of Dourbies cemetery the GR follows the road on the left to Le Viala, and then a track westwards along a hill with a reservoir on top. It joins the draille, the old road from Dourbies to Meyrueis, and after a long climb followed by a series of hairpin bends reaches the Col du Suquet at 1,280m. The draille crosses the Haut-Suquet forestry track 200 metres north of the col, and then turns sharply to the east.

Alternative route via GR66A, Col du Suquet to Pierre Plantée via Camprieu. The long empty stage from Dourbies to Meyrueis can be divided in two at the cost of a deviation via Camprieu, where both accommodation and provisions are available. This also gives the opportunity to visit the caverns at Bramabiau.

The Alternative route to Camprieu, waymarked as GR66A, starts from a point on the Dourbies

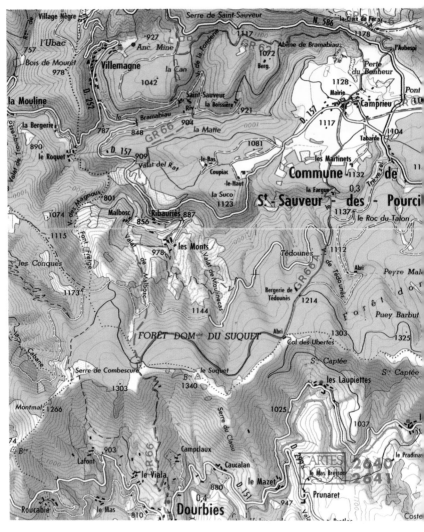

6.5Km
1:45

to Meyrueis stretch of the GR66 some 200 metres north of the Col du Suquet.

From the point of separation the GR66A heads north west on the Haut-Suquet forestry road, as it winds through beechwoods on the northern slope of the Montagne du Suquet, 1,340m, to reach the Col des Ubertes, where there is a hut. At a meeting of paths 500 metres to the north east of this col, at altitude mark 1,214m,

The Periglacial Climate: A Case of Solifluction
No incontrovertible evidence of glaciers has been found on the Aigoual massif. The 'Trépaloup moraine' is no doubt only a particular case of the colluvial movements which covered the slopes of the massif with a layer of deposits that in places is very thick. One instance of solifluction is worth noting. On the north flank of the Montagne du Suquet certain thalwegs where the slope is fairly gentle are littered with blocks of sandstone, many of them as much as a cubic metre in size, deriving from the mountain's infra-liassic mantle. Below the permanently frozen subsoil (the permafrost) a semi-liquid mud brought about by the summer thaws then slipped down the slight slopes and left a coating on these sandstone blocks.

CAMPRIEU
🏠 ⛺ 🏕 🍴 🍷 ⛲ 🚌
1,090m
Junction with the GR62.
Abîme de Bramabiau, north west of Camprieu on GR62: limestone caverns and galleries where Bonheur stream emerges from its underground course. May be open in summer on occasions when river waters are low. Enquiries regarding access should be made to the Guides' House alongside the N586.

6.5Km
1:45

Junction
The GR6 coming from Mont Aigoual and Prat-Peirot joins the GR66A at the Croix-de-Fer.

take the left-hand track. Then, 300 metres farther on, go down to the left on a footpath which joins the Suquet road where it crosses the Tédounès stream. Follow this road to the right. After 200 metres fork left on to a track which leaves the road and runs down northwards through woods to a footbridge over the Trévezel, just before the hamlet of La Fargue. On reaching the houses take the old track on the left which skirts around a meadow, climbs up on to the plateau, veers northward again and brings you to Camprieu.

From the Camprieu mairie the GR66A climbs up to the Croix-du-Puech, at first sharing the same route as the GR62, and passes above the 'perte du Bonheur' where the stream runs underground.

A little farther on the GR62 forks left, northwards, towards the Bramabiau Guides' House. The GR66A forks right towards the isolated Aubespi farm, crosses the N586, skirts around the farm and climbs up to the Col de la Croix-de-Fer, at 1,178m, by the old Valleraugue to Meyrueis road, which is also followed by the GR6.

The 2 GRs continue together on the old road, which is still motorable, running along the southern flank of La Fajolle. Reaching the crest it crosses over for a few hundred metres to the northern slope of the Serre de Saint-Sauveur. Farther to the west a footpath comes in from

the left; this is the old Saint-Sauveur to Lanuéjols road which is followed by the GR66 and GR62.

Junction

The GR66A, with the GR6, rejoins the GR66 coming from Dourbies and the Col du Suquet, and the GR62.

At this point the GR66A comes to an end. Some 400 metres farther on to the north west the GR62 turns off the old Meyrueis road to follow the so-called 'Traberse' of Lanuéjols, while the GR66 and GR6 go on together towards Meyrueis from the junction known as

---

Bramabiau (the 'Bull-roarer')

It was in the Liassic seas at the start of the Secondary area that the limestone deposits were laid down, in which the Bramabiau caverns would eventually be hollowed out. Towards the middle of the Tertiary period the region suffered a series of dislocations, and today the Suquet massif, tilted towards the north, only retains its Secondary covering at the point where the great east/west fault separates it from the Aigoual, on the small Camprieu causse. As already described, the Bonheur stream disappears through the Balset swallowhole, and runs through deep and narrow galleries, to reach daylight again through the impressive fissure at Bramabiau.

In 1888 Edouard Martel, pioneer of speleology, first attempted the underground journey. He and a few friends travelled upstream in a collapsible boat, surmounting a series of cascades and taking 3 hours to achieve their objective. Construction works undertaken in 1925 in the interests of safety have enabled excursions through the grottos to be arranged in summer, on occasions when the waters are low.

---

the 'Pierre Plantée'.

Col du Suquet
1,280m
GR66 junction with GR66A

From the Col du Suquet north of Dourbies. The GR66 descends northwards to the Suquet road at altitude mark 1,159m where, 50 metres to the west, there is a water point. It continues down a footpath opposite, and after a sharp elbow-bend to the east, reaches Les Monts hamlet at 970m. Skirting the hamlet to the north the GR, close to the bridge over the Trévezel, joins the road climbing westwards along the right bank of the stream. Shortly after the fork leading to Ribauriès the GR follows the old road on the right from Les Monts to Saint-Sauveur-des-Pourcils, climbing parallel to the road, to reach the D157 road.

6Km

D157 Road

The GR crosses the D157 and continues to climb, first through a clearing, then into the forest, and crosses the Valat-du-Rat. It joins the forestry road no. 1 at altitude mark 904m shortly before the Pont de l'Ane over the Bramabiau stream. A narrow path climbs up from the bridge into the valley of the Fonderie stream leaving it on the left for the church at Saint-Sauveur-des-Pourcils and the forester's lodge at 930m. From the wayside cross the GR climbs directly north along the old Saint-Sauveur-des-Pourcils road to Lanuéjols and the forestry road no. 1 again.

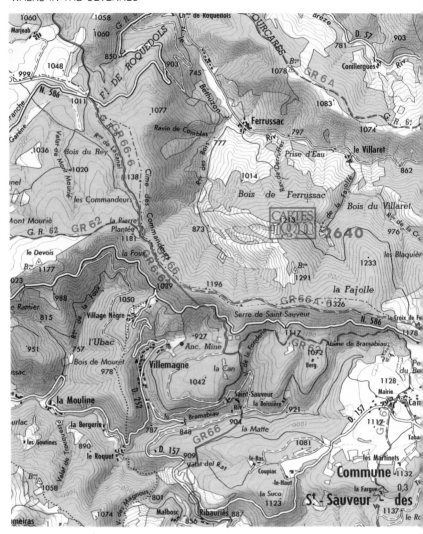

5Km

The GR62 from Camprieu joins the GR66 and follows the same route as far as La Pierre Plantée.

Junction

The GR66A alternative route and the GR6, following the old road from Valleraugue to

The GR follows the forestry road as far as the N586 at the Michelin marker. It crosses the road to a footpath and continues along it north westwards to the old road from Valleraugue to Meyrueis.

The GR66, with GRs 62 and 6, continues on the old road to the crossroads called La Pierre Plantée.

Forests on Mont Aigoual

The history of forest development on this massif since the last ice age has been traced from pollen analyses of soil at the higher altitudes. Though not englaciated, the Aigoual was subject to intense periglacial action which wiped out the trees. In subsequent warm periods development followed much the same pattern as on Mont Lozère, though here walnut as well as oak followed the birch, with holm-oak hard on their heels in intensely hot dry periods that coincided with the Chalcolithic. From the Bronze Age onward, cooler and damper conditions favoured the beech, soon destroyed however, presumably because sheep farmers of the Garrigues not only opened up great pathways for movement of flocks, but burned down huge areas of beechwoods to extend the grazing on both Mont Aigoual and the Lingas. And so it went on. In the 18th century some 30,000 sheep were said to be on the heights of this massif; and the needs of factories, foundries and mines for timber hastened the deforestation, until near the end of the Second Empire only some 2,000 hectares of beechwoods remained.

Meyrueis, join the GR66 and GR62 on the right.

La Pierre Plantée

1,170m
The GR62 separates from the GR66 and GR6 on the left at the crossroads, following the track called the 'Traberse' of Lanuéjols to the east. The GR66 and GR6 continue on the same route following the old road from Valleraugue as far as Meyrueis.

6Km
1:30

The GR descends through forest for about 2 kilometres and crosses the N586 at the 'Haut-de-Côte' at altitude mark 1,011m on the borders of the Gard and the Lozére departments and on the edge of the Causse Noir. The GR returns to the old road opposite for about 500 metres and then, at the first hairpin bend, it leaves the road for a path on the left which climbs up to a track passing close to Marjoab. After almost 3 kilometres along the left bank of the Valat-de-la-Vinade

Reafforestation of Mont Aigoual

Here too the expertise and devotion of Georges Fabre led, between 1874 and 1908, to restoration of the remaining woodland on the Aigoual massif and replanting - in all, 16,000 hectares of state forests including 3,000 hectares of protective trees and 11,000 for timber production. The aim was to produce a carefully planned mixed woodland, with conifers rather than beech on the south facing slopes. Experimental arboretums led to successful acclimatisation of fast-growing species, as at the Hort de Dieu, 200 metres below the Observatory on Mont Aigoual itself, and at La Foux where Douglas firs 42 metres in height and 2.70 metres in circumference were achieved. The timber trade has continued to flourish, two-thirds of production going to the Union Forestière Viganaise, selling through a sawmill at Le Vigan. There are also sawmills at Meyrueis, and wood pulp is re-sold to paper mills, including one at Arles.

FROM P. MARRES AND R. VACQUIER

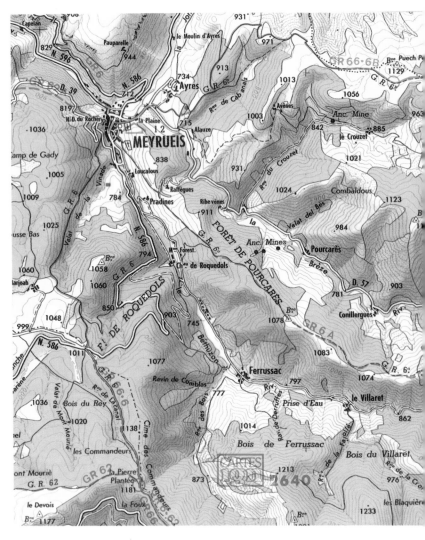

the GR reaches Meyrueis at the confluence of La Jonte, La Brèze and Le Béthuzon.

MEYRUEIS

700m

The estimated walking time for the 13km to Cabrillac is 4 hrs.

The GR leaves Meyrueis northwards over the Béthuzon bridge, turning right in front of the chemist's shop, and after about 500 metres crosses the Brèze where it flows into the Jonte. On the right bank the GR follows the old track to Ayres, between the Ayres road and the D57, but leaves it soon on the right, climbing up

The northern section of the GR66, some 23 kilometres between Meyrueis and Aire-de-Côte, is a picturesque region but also an empty region with few places where provisions or accommodation can be found, although, about halfway, at Cabrillac, there is a well-known

5Km

through a series of hairpin bends in a more or less north easterly direction. Beyond the holiday village it enters the forest, then after a hairpin bend skirts the hill at altitude mark 913m in a westward direction and emerges into open country. The track skirts the head of the Ravin de Cabanais, and bearing eastwards again, reaches the Crouzet forest at the foot of Puech Pounchut.

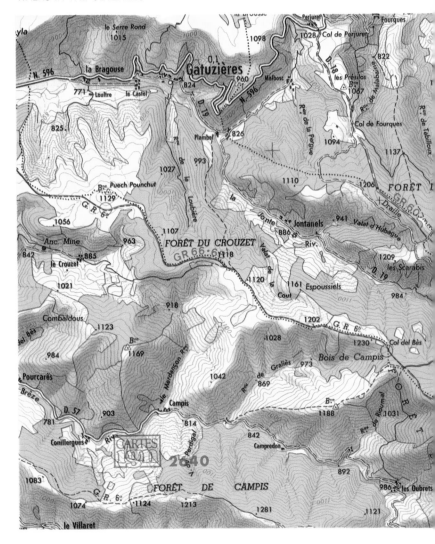

restaurant and 500 metres
farther east, a gîte d'étape.
From Meyrueis to Cabrillac
and to Aire-de-Côte the way
is pleasant and without
difficulty along old and little
frequented paths.
The GR6 separates from the
GR66 northwards. The GR66
and GR6B follow the same

The Château de Roquedols

In the foothills of Mont Aigoual, 2 kilometres upstream from Meyrueis in the lower Béthuzon valley, this château seems reluctant to show itself, huddled against the forest at the end of a long drive. Its history is unclear. The date 1534 appears over the main door, but the building is certainly older. However the names of all its owners since the early 17th century are known, ending with the Forestry Commission in 1938. Used in 1943/44 as a depository for the collections of national museums, and then as a youth camp, it reverted after the Liberation to the Forestry Commission, which made it over to the National Park in 1972.

The house itself is very pleasing. Its 2 wings forming a right angle and linked together by 3 round towers, with an attractive interior courtyard, are built of pinkish sandstone weathered to a warm tint that stands out from the forest behind and above.

Today the first floor provides quarters for some of the National Park staff, while the main ground floor rooms and library have been restored for use as exhibition halls. In 1977 the Park decided to turn these into an 'interpretation centre' relating to the history, geography and socio-economic development of the Aigoual massif, with indoor exhibitions complemented by a short circular walk in the neighbouring forest, to illustrate the work of the Park and acquaint people with the various types of trees.

route from Meyrueis to a crossroads at Col del Bès.

Puech Pounchut
1,129m

5Km

Col del Bès
At the crossways the GR6B separates from the GR66 and continues to the south east towards L'Aigoual.

3Km

The GR continues along the old track from Meyrueis to Cabrillac and goes in amongst the beautiful beech groves of the Crouzet forest, following close to the mountain ridge between altitude marks 1,107m and 1,118m. At altitude mark 1,120m it crosses a broad col known as Peyremoula (from *pierre à meule* meaning a millstone) notable for a bed of sandstone, all that remains of the covering of the Secondary era worn away by erosion. The GR continues on the old road eastwards between altitude marks 1,202m and 1,230m, now in the open, now in the forest, following the ridge separating the valley of the Jonte to the north from the valley of the Brèze to the south. Soon after the 1,230 altitude mark it reaches a crossways called Col del Bès on the map, with a large beech tree nearby.

The GR66, still following the old track from Meyrueis, turns eastwards, to the left, along the northern slope of the Montagne de Malacrème, 1,399m high, then descends into the Jonte valley. It crosses the river by a stone bridge

117

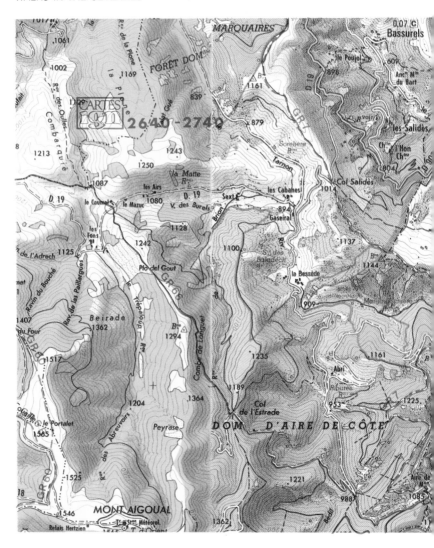

and climbs up again afterwards to Cabrillac.

CABRILLAC

△ ✕ ☖

1,200m

*The estimated walking time
for the 10km to Aire-de-Côte
is 3 hrs 15 mins.
The GR66 intersects the line
of the 'Grande Draille', the*

From the crossroads to the east of the hamlet the GR initially follows the D19 road eastwards, but after some 50 metres it leaves the road for the old track to Saint-André-de-Valborgne on the left. The track, parallel to the road at first, passes close by a *gîte d'étape*, then following the borders of the Rousses and Bassurels Communes it reaches the Trépaloup stream.

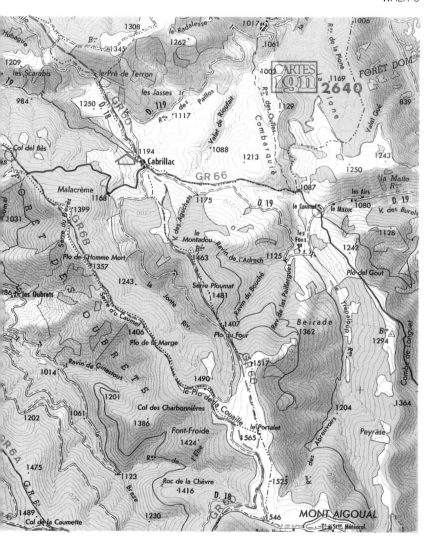

2Km

Draille d'Aubrac. Climbing from L'Espérou to the Col de Prat-Peirot, the draille crosses to the west from the summits of L'Aigoual, descends to Le Plo del Four, passes close by Le Serre Ploumat, and slopes down towards Cabrillac. The draille sets off again to the north

The GR crosses the stream over a stone bridge and climbs up afterwards towards the isolated Caumel farm, below which it passes to reach and cross the D19 road.

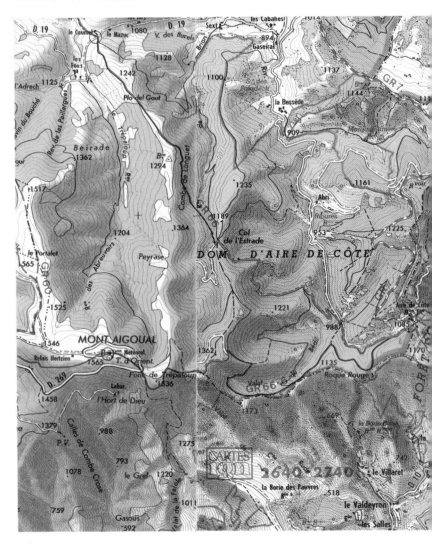

*west followed at first by the
D18 road. They separate and
the draille goes on, higher
up in the forest, to the Col
de Perjuret.*

Caumel

From the D19 in front of the Caumel farm the
GR climbs to the south east and follows the
old track from Cabrillac to Saint-Marcel-de-
Fontfouillouse. At first, climbing southwards

8Km

AIRE-DE-CÔTE
⌂

1,085m
Junction The GRs 6, 7, 66
and 67 meet at the forester's
lodge. The GR6 and GR7
follow the same route
westwards as the GR66 as
far as the Col de Prat-Peirot.

7Km
2:30

MONT AIGOUAL
⌂ ⌂ ⍾

1,565m

along a long ridge cut by the col, Le Plo del Gout, 1,223m, the GR enters the forest a little to the north of altitude mark 1,294m and follows the western slope of the Brion valley. It descends among the beeches in the forest for about 2 kilometres, crosses a small stream, and then reaches the ford on the Brion stream - easy to cross in good weather. The GR then climbs up through a hairpin bend to the Col de l'Estrade at 1,180m where the track becomes suitable for motor vehicles and continues in a generally south eastern direction. At the first salient it passes by the Pouset track on the right, and farther on, the track to Aire-de-Côte via the Bidil valley. After a hairpin bend the GR reaches the high valley of the Tarnon at altitude mark 988m and climbs the road following the valley to the Aire-de-Côte forester's lodge.

The GR leaves by the Bessède road south westwards and after 200 metres follows a motor road on the left for about 2 kilometres. At the point where the road descends steeply towards the Bidil ravine - the scene of a tragedy involving the Aire-de-Côte maquis in 1943 - the GR leaves it for a path on the left which skirts the head of the ravine and leads to another motor road. The GR at first follows the road to the west towards the Atlantic/Mediterranean watershed overlooking the Hérault valley. Then after a deviation northwards it emerges from the forest in sight of the Observatoire de L'Aigoual to proceed directly across the northern slope of the Pic de la Fajole, 1,536m high, to the Col de Trépaloup. It is, however, better to leave the GR and skirt the Pic de la Fajole to the south by the sentier des Botanistes, providing some very fine views, and join the Col de Trépaloup. Cross the D269 road to reach Mont Aigoual and the observatory.

From the observatory car park the GR crosses the D269 road and follows the old Aigoual track westwards, descending the southern slope of the mountain *en corniche*. It reaches the new road, not shown on the map, linking the Prat-Peirot car park with the D269, crosses it and descends towards the D269. Just before reaching the road the GR follows a ski track on

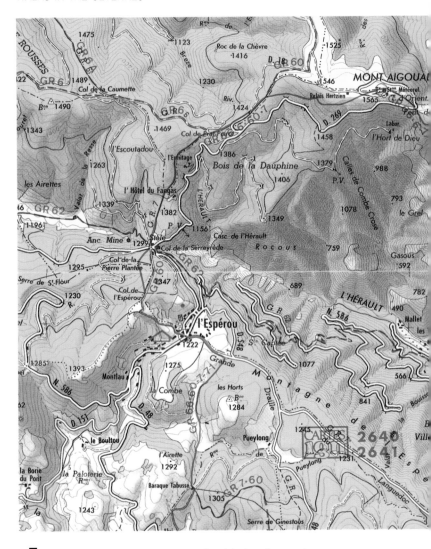

the right heading south west.

The GR60 from Cabrillac joins the GRs 6, 7 and 66.

The ski track crosses the D18 which leads to the Prat-Peirot chalets.

The GR6 separates from the GR66 and GR7 at the Col de Prat-Peirot and goes north west towards the Col de la Caumette.

The GR66 joins the draille which descends for 2 kilometres to the south west and then southwards to the Col de la Serreyrède.

The Hérault Valley

The upper valley of the River Hérault has sliced deep into the Aigoual massif. Though its source is perched at nearly 1,400m, it is at 1,300m, level with the Col de la Serreyrède, where it is known as the Valat de Serreyrède, that it really starts to carve out its great trench, with the higher branch of the Hérault coming in from above at 1,800m, dropping through a series of falls.

Once formed, the upper Hérault valley comprises 2 sections. The upstream section runs in a straight line from west to east for 8 or 9 kilometres, as far as the confluence of the Clarou, where the stream bed is no higher than 350m. The lower one heads from north west to south east as far as Le Mazel, then makes a bend and runs directly from north to south, to reach the confluence with the Arre at 181m. Along the upstream section the gradient is only about 1 in 11, but between the Valat de Serreyrède and the Valat de Bertel it can steepen to about 1 in 4, as the Hérault has to contend with great boulders blocking its path. For 2.5 kilometres it drops so swiftly through the Rocoux gorges that the tributary waters here only reach it downstream from their confluence points, which remain suspended above. This steepening of the river's longitudinal profile and that of its tributaries accelerates its torrential flow, already exacerbated by the extraordinarily heavy rainstorms that hit these hillsides.

The fact that this section of the valley is virtually enclosed in a cutting for a whole kilometre explains the sheltered climate it enjoys, with very high temperatures and sunshine levels in spring and summer. A few holm-oaks cling to the *adrets* above Valleraugue, up to 950m. The area above the steeper slopes is covered in forests replanted since 1880, consisting, on the *ubacs* side, of chestnut up to 800m. Above that a stretch of open moorland with broom separates the chestnut from the realm of beech, now mingled with stands of fir, spruce and larch.

6.5Km
1:45

The Col de la Serreyrède is a crossroads of exceptional importance; situated on the watershed it presents the classic spectacle of the contrast between the deep ravine of the Hérault and the tranquil valley of the Bonheur stream. From time immemorial, the Draille d'Aubrac has taken this route with its famous and splendid water source rushing down the steep slope both to the north and to the south.

At the col the GR takes the path called 'de Max' that leaves the D269 to the south. A few steps west of the crossroads it follows a pleasant route in the forest, rejoins the draille at the Col de l'Espérou and follows it to L'Espérou.

L'ESPÉROU

ACCOMMODATION GUIDE

The many different kinds of accommodation in France are explained in the introduction. Here we include a selection of hotels and other addresses, which is by no means exhaustive – the hotels listed are usually in the one-star or two-star categories. We have given full postal addresses where available so bookings can be made.

There has been an explosive growth in bed and breakfast facilities *(chambres d'hôte)* in the past few years, and staying in these private homes can be especially interesting and rewarding. Local shops and the town hall *(mairie)* can usually direct you to one.

Aigoual (Mont)
30570 Valleraugue
⌂
☎ 67.82.62.78 and
67.82.22.78

Aire-de-Côte
48400 Bassurels
⌂
M. Garcia
☎ 66.44.70.47

Anduze
30140 Anduze
⌂
M.F. Grendene
11 Rue du Luxembourg
☎ 66.61.70.27

Auriac
⌂
☎ 66.47.64.72

Ayres
48150 Meyrueis
⌂
M. Poujols
☎ 66.45.62.73

Ayres (Les)
48240
⌂
M. Larguier
☎ 66.45.90.26
⌂
M. Imbert
☎ 66.45.90.95

Bagnols-les-Bains
⌂ La Chaumière
☎ 66.47.60.18
⌂ du Commerce
☎ 66.47.60.07
⌂ Moderne

☎ 66.47.60.04
⌂ du Pont
☎ 66.47.60.03

Barre-des-Cévennes
48400
⌂
M. Combes
☎ 66.45.05.28

La Bessède
30122 Les Plantiers
⌂
M. Victor
☎ 66.83.92.32

Le Bleymard
⌂ La Remise
☎ 66.48.65.80
⌂ Chalet du Mont Lozère
☎ 66.48.62.84

Cabrillac
48150
⌂ ARCL
30190 Sauzet
M. Issartel
☎ 66.81.62.64

Campmau
30140 Mialet
⌂
M. Clément
☎ 66.55.60.64

Camprieu
30750
⌂
☎ 67.82.61.20

Col de Jalcreste
48240
⌂
M. Baï

☎ 66.45.04.93

Colognac
⌂
M. Chartreux
Place de la Mairie
☎ 66.85.28.84
⌂ Le Guralier
Mme Desvignes
☎ 66.85.23.28

Concoules
⌂ Beauséjour
☎ 66.83.72.43

Croix de Berthel
⌂ Auberge Les Bastides
Mme Clavel
☎ 66.45.81.35

Cubières
⌂ Bargeton
☎ 66.48.62.54

Dourbies
30750
⌂
M. Balsan
67.82.71.95
⌂ Auberge
67.82.70.88 and 67.88.77.67

L'Espérou
30570
⌂
M. Carayon
Route de Valleraugue
☎ 67.82.60.14

La Fage
⌂
☎ 66.48.05.36

Florac
⌂ Central
☎ 66.45.00.01
⌂ des Gorges du Tarn
☎ 66.45.00.63
⌂ du Parc
☎ 66.45.03.05
⌂ Ponsolle
☎ 66.45.01.38
42400 Florac
⌂
Mme Rives
Rue de l'Église
☎ 66.45.14.93
⌂
M. Serran
Le Pont du Tarn
☎ 66.45.05.51
⌂ Old Presbytery
M. Martinez
18 Rue du Pêcheur
☎ 66.45.24.54

Gourdouse
See Vialas

L'Hospitalet
48400 Vebron
⌂
Mme Pin
Ferme de l'Hospitalet
☎ 66.44.01.60

Lasalle
30460
⌂ Parc des Glycines
Mme Cros
Lamouthe
☎ 66.85.21.31

Marjoabè
48150 Meyrueis

⌂
M.G. Libourel
☎ 66.45.64.18

Mas de la Barque
⌂ Ski-Club Alèsien
☎ 66.46.80.28

Le Mazel
48190 Bagnols-les-Bains
⌂
☎ 66.48.61.38

Meyrueis
See Ayres and Marjoab

Mialet
See Campmau

Mijavols
⌂ Barn
M. Chaptal Héli
☎ 66.45.09.04

Le Pendédis
48160
⌂
M. Pascal
☎ 66.45.52.03

Pont de Burgen
48330
⌂
Mme Donnet
☎ 66.45.73.94

Pont de Montvert
⌂ Les Cévennes
☎ 66.45.80.01
⌂ Sources du Tarn
☎ 66.45.80.25
⌂ Auberge de la Regalière

☎ 66.45.81.65

La Pigeire
48800 Altier
⌂
M. Moulin-Collinet
☎ 66.46.81.65

Les Plantiers
30122
⌂
M. Stumpf
☎ 66.83.91.25

Saint-Germain-de-Calberte
48370
⌂
Mme Fabre
☎ 66.45.91.55

Serre de la Can
48370 St-Germain-de-Calberte
⌂
☎ 66.45.90.06

Valleraugue
30570
⌂
M. Viau
Foyer Rural
☎ 67.82.20.08

Vialas
⌂ Chantoiseau
☎ 66.45.04.02

Villefort
48800
⌂ Les Sédariès
☎ 66.46.84.33

INDEX

Details of bus/train connections have been provided wherever it was possible. We suggest you refer also to the map inside the front cover.